Business Intelligence: The IBM Solution

T0183727

Springer
London
Berlin
Heidelberg
New York
Barcelona
Hong Kong
Milan
Paris
Santa Clara
Singapore
Tokyo

Mark Whitehorn
University College Worcester, Worcester UK

Mary Whitehorn
Penguinsoft Ltd, Bromyard, UK

ISBN 1-85233-085-6 Springer-Verlag London Berlin Heidelberg

British Library Cataloguing in Publication Data
Whitehorn, Mark
 Business Intelligence : the IBM solution : data warehousing
 and OLAP
 1.Data warehousing 2. Decision support systems 3.Business
 intelligence – Data processing
 I.Title II.Whitehorn, Mary
 658.4'038'0285'5365
 ISBN 1852330856

Library of Congress Cataloging-in-Publication Data
Whitehorn, Mark, 1953–
 Business intelligence : the IBM solution : datawarehousing and
 OLAP / Mark Whitehorn and Mary Whitehorn.
  p. cm.
 Includes index.

 Additional material to this book can be downloaded from http://extras.springer.com.

 ISBN 1-85233-085-6 (alk. paper)
 1. Data warehousing. 2. Online data processing. 3. Business
 intelligence. I. Whitehorn, Mary, 1959– . II. Title.
 QA76.9.D37W482 1999
 658.4'038'0285574--dc21   98-32313

Typeset by Ian Kingston Editorial Services, Nottingham, UK
Printed and bound by the Creative Print & Design Group (Wales), Ebbw Vale
34/3830-543210 Printed on acid-free paper

Business Intelligence: The IBM Solution

Mark Whitehorn and Mary Whitehorn

Springer

Acknowledgements

We were privileged to spend a week at IBM's Santa Teresa laboratories and also some time at the IBM site in Warwick, England. In both places we were able to talk to the people who develop this software, to others who install it for major customers and to those who train people to use it effectively. Everyone we met was enormously encouraging, helpful and gave generously of their time and expertise. We have tried to incorporate accurately their suggestions, tips and tweaks into this book so when you come across something that sounds suspiciously well informed, the credit goes to those guys rather than to us. If there are mistakes, blame us; it is our book, after all.

As we said, everyone was helpful but particular thanks must go to Alan Carpenter (IBM Warwick) for his cogent comments and appreciation of what we were trying to achieve.

Grateful thanks also go to (in alphabetical order)

Gary Robinson – Santa Teresa   Gil Lee – Santa Teresa
Holly Rader – Santa Teresa   Iain Allen – Warwick
Julie Filip – Santa Teresa   Ron Bingham – Santa Teresa
Susan Fisher – Santa Teresa   Tom Lockwood – Santa Teresa

Shaun Jones, Adrian Slater and Mike Blake (IBM) and Beverley Ford and Rebecca Moore (Springer-Verlag) all worked hard behind the scenes and provided the drive; without their enthusiasm and vision you certainly wouldn't be reading this book.

We'd also like to extend a huge thank you to Andy and Steve Marra (and Sophie and Ross) for the generous loan of their Truckee home. There, in the peace and quiet amongst the trees, we roughed out the framework of the book.

In like vein, thanks also go to Colin and Sue Clark at the Wheelwrights, Pencombe, for providing another home from home and excellent comestibles.

Finally, a big thank you to our proof-readers, Helen Arthan and Mark Burton, and she of the purple pen (ta, Ma).

Mark Whitehorn
Mary Whitehorn

Contents

Contents

Introduction

Who are you?

It seems reasonable, given the title of the book, to assume that you're looking at it because you have an interest in IBM's Business Intelligence tools (specifically Visual Warehouse and DB2 OLAP Server) or Business Intelligence in general. If not, you may have picked up the wrong book. If you are in a bookstore, whatever you do don't pay for it yet: find a quiet corner and read this introduction. It tells you what the prospective readers are like and what they can expect from the book. On the other hand, if you know exactly what this book is about and why you are reading it (perhaps your boss put it on your desk with a note "There will be questions on Monday") you may well be advised to skip straight to Chapter 1 and get started.

This book was written for two flavors of reader:

- A DBA (Database Administrator) who has just been told to become a DWA (Data Warehouse Administrator).
- A manager involved in decisions about how data is to be organized within an enterprise.

Both of these readers need information about Business Intelligence. The former needs background information about what Business Intelligence is and what the tools can do, and also how to drive the software. The latter needs the same overview without the hands-on element. This book provides both sorts of information.

In practice, job definitions within the IT industry are notoriously inexact and there is often a fair degree of overlap between 'line of business' and 'database administration' decision-makers in organizations of all sizes. Both managers (in the traditional sense) and DBAs may need to be involved in data-handling decisions and, indeed, it can be argued that the best decisions are those that take account of both these viewpoints.

So, no matter who you are, if you want an overview of Business Intelligence in general and IBM's solution in particular, we recommend that you read:

Chapter 1 – Do You Need Business Intelligence?

Appendix 1 – Overview of Data Warehousing

Chapter 13 – OLAP Concepts and Terminology

Chapter 19 – Anchor Dimensions and a Few More Concepts and Pointers

Chapter 20 – Visual Warehouse and DB2 OLAP Server Symbiosis

Appendix 2 – IBM's Business Intelligence Solution

If you need to learn how to use IBM's Business Intelligence tools, we recommend that you start here at the beginning.

What this book does

This book does two things: it provides a conceptual overview of Business Intelligence and its core components – data warehousing and On-Line Analytical Processing (OLAP) – and it explains the steps necessary for a first implementation.

In both the Visual Warehouse and DB2 OLAP Server sections we start with an overview of what the application has to offer; we also include any background issues or underlying concepts that help to pull the overview into focus. We then take a step-by-step path through the processes required to get a very simple system working. After this, further steps explore some of the functionality that gives the application its power, and this completes the fast start.

Above all, this is a "get you up and running in the shortest possible time" book. It certainly won't tell you every last detail about the products but it will take you on a rapid path through the installation and early experimentation stages, to a point from which you can launch yourself into a deeper understanding.

We won't be covering every detail because the guys at IBM are much better qualified to do this, as the manuals bear witness. These are excellent, packed with all the information and detail you could ever need. The trouble with those heavyweight (in terms of actual mass as well as content) tomes is that it is often difficult to filter out the minimum information required when you're starting out with a product. At that stage you don't need to know all the variations on a theme, you just need the information that is most likely to be relevant. What we've done is to extract that information and present it in what is hopefully an easily digestible form.

Our approach

We've based this book on our own experience of tackling new software. We usually don't have time to go on a course, nor to sit and read the manuals first; instead we install the software, play with it, install some test data, play with that and so on. After a while we develop a sense of how the software works. At that point we go back to the beginning, throw away all of the work so far and get started with some real prototype data – data that actually applies to the problem we are trying to solve. We play with that for a while, and all the time we're learning the software. Finally, we start yet again, this time for real, and try to build something that actually solves problems.

We think our behaviour is perfectly normal and that many people work like this, so we've structured the book to complement this approach. For example, this is the first view you get of Visual Warehouse; where do you begin?

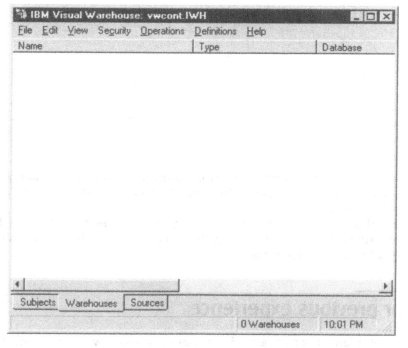

The answer, surprisingly, is to go to the third tab at the bottom (Sources), and choose File, New.

Another problem is that it is often unclear what bits of the software are vital to get it working and which bits can safely be left for later study. For example, this is the second dialog box that you reach after selecting File, New from the Sources tab.

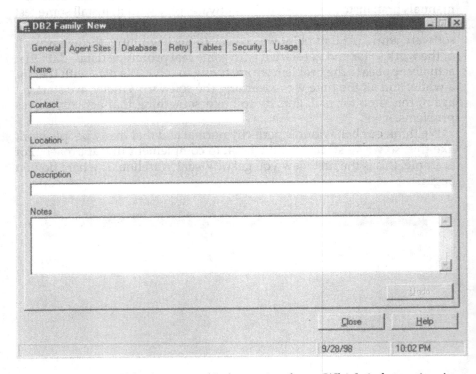

There are seven tabbed pages of information here. Which information is vital, what can be left during a first run through and where is it safe to accept the defaults?

We had to discover all this, so to speed your progress we've plotted the easiest path to getting started and, on the way, have identified what is vital and what you can leave for the present.

Your previous experience

If you do plan to set up and drive these products, we have made the assumption that you are familiar with databases in general, with the relational model, normalization and its implications, and that you can drive DB2 and are conversant with SQL. Here we will shamelessly plug our two earlier publications, 'Inside Relational Databases' by Mark Whitehorn and Bill Marklyn (ISBN 3-540-76092-X, Springer-Verlag) and 'DB2 for Windows NT – Fast' by the present authors (ISBN 3-540-76200-0, Springer-Verlag). These two books aim to get people up to speed with these subjects and are useful reading if our assumptions above are incorrect.

So do you need this book?

We feel it's worthwhile being clear about what we can offer.

- An overview of what Business Intelligence has to offer? – This we can do.
- How to install the products, specifically Visual Warehouse and DB2 OLAP Server, to run under Windows NT? – Certainly.
- How to get over that first, steep learning curve? – Yes.
- How to get prototype sets of data installed and working? – Yes.
- Every last tip and trick to make your data warehouse run that little bit faster when the wind's from the South? – No.
- Strategies for using these tools to improve your business specifically? – Absolutely not (we wouldn't have the temerity to tell you how best to run your business).

Disclaimer

Life's complicated, and the arena of data management is even more so. While we have made every effort to ensure that the contents of this book are accurate, we cannot take responsibility for any errors, glitches or disasters you may encounter in your experience of the products we cover. The variation between different hardware, software, networking and data storage setups renders it an impossible task to guarantee that something will work under all circumstances. The responsibility for the integrity of systems and data is in the hands of the people who work with it. We'll help all we can, but be careful out there.

Backup

What can we tell you that you haven't heard before? Back up your data.

Happily, backing up skills gained using DB2 will transfer to backing up your data warehouse and any OLAP implementation, as DB2 underlies both these technologies. If you're not familiar with DB2 backup procedures, there's a comprehensive section in the aforementioned book, 'DB2 for Windows NT – Fast'.

Yo IBM (or 'Nobody was ever fired for buying IBM')

IBM was extremely helpful in providing us with the facilities we needed to write this book. However, we have no shares in IBM, nor does the company have any editorial control whatsoever over the content of this book. So, in our opinion, is it worth looking at IBM's products for Business Intelligence?

The simple answer is a resounding 'Yes'. We are in the happy position of being able to choose the books that we write. We don't write books about products that we don't actually like or trust.

It is true that there are cheaper products around, and there are products with better, more intuitive interfaces. That's the bad news. The good news is that IBM's Business Intelligence tools are extremely robust. IBM's understanding of data handling is second to none, and is an excellent basis for such complex tools. Given the choice between a pretty face and robust handling of data, there is no doubt which is more important.

Another major point in IBM's favor is the scalability issue. The sky's the limit, which is just as well considering the quantum leaps in data size that can occur. Data warehouses are famous for growing, and OLAP solutions even more so, making scalability an important factor. You need never have nightmares about having nowhere to go if order-of-magnitude expansionist plans suddenly materialize.

In addition, IBM's Business Intelligence products are also immensely strong in areas such as automating processes intelligently, data transformation, data summation, process documentation, etc.

Don't buy Visual Warehouse if you are intending to set up a very simple, non-mission critical data warehouse based upon one operational database. In all other cases, we heartily recommend that you consider it as a serious option. We can't tell you that it is the right choice for your business, only that it is always on the list of options that we present to clients.

Versioning

In the production of this book we used the beta code release of Visual Warehouse 5.2 and of DB2 OLAP Server 1.0.1, and also the previous versions (Visual Warehouse 3.1 and DB2 OLAP Server 1.0).

Whenever possible we've used the most recent versions, but in some instances the screen shots may differ very slightly from what you see on screen. We've also noted, where it seems helpful, changes that have occurred between these releases.

Who should you be?

❛ *Given the first sub-heading of this chapter, this seems a fitting one with which to end.* ❜

During the course of this book, we'll be using multiple products – Windows NT, DB2, Visual Warehouse, DataGuide, DB2 OLAP Server, Essbase – and all require you to identify yourself with a user ID and password. Some restrict the length of password, some are case sensitive and some aren't. To keep things simple and to avoid potential conflicts, we have used the same identity throughout the installations and examples in this book.

We started by creating an NT user with administrator rights called mark with a password of between six and eight characters. (*Yes, we are too paranoid to tell you what the password was.*) We used this user whenever creating databases in DB2, installing new software, whatever.

Then, every time we installed the next bit of software, we used this same ID and password. We don't recommend that you use 'Mark'; in fact, we recommend that you don't. However, we do recommend that you choose, right from the start, a user that matches the following conditions – an ID of eight characters or fewer and a password of between six and eight characters. The password must also obey the NT conventions (no spaces etc.). We also recommend that you note the case of both ID and password, and always duplicate them exactly.

If you stick to these rules, then you should then be able to use this ID for all of the software described here. If you don't then you may find that a password which works for one system fails for another (for example, Essbase tolerates longer passwords than NT).

Of course, this advice is designed to keep things simple when you are learning the software on a test system. You may well want to develop a more complex set of IDs when you start to develop a system for real.

Chapter 1

Do you need Business Intelligence?

Do you need Business Intelligence?

If spelled without the capital letters, the answer would surely be an un-qualified yes, but as soon as we add the capitalization (and the words suddenly refer to a particular type of software) it's a different ball game.

What we think you have

You, or rather your company, will have at least one operational database, and very likely more than one – an 'operational database' in this sense is defined as one that's used to store company information, with data being added, changed, browsed and extracted on a minute-by-minute or at least hour-by-hour basis.

These databases are likely to be located on different host machines running different operating systems (anything from DOS and Windows to AIX, VMS and Unix) and in DBMSs ranging from Approach and Access to Oracle and DB2. The host machines are probably linked by a network so that it's possible to see all of the databases from one location.

Remember, size isn't important

The amount of data stored in the database or databases is not particularly important at this point. Some companies hold terabytes of data, others hold a few megabytes. The survival of a company can depend on its data, regardless of the amount stored, and to the people involved, the survival of a small company is just as important as that of a large corporation.

Problems addressed by Business Intelligence software

If you have no problems with data, everything in your business is running smoothly, and everyone in the organization can always get the data they need at a moment's notice, then you don't need Business Intelligence. A tool is only useful if it solves a problem and/or lets you achieve something that's impossible at present. Business Intelligence tools have arisen to solve a whole class of problems that afflict those who use data within an organization, and these problems fall into three broad categories.

1. Questions that span time

Managers in your organization need answers to simple questions like "How many tins of cat food have we sold in the past five years?" This type of question isn't, of itself, a problem. However, if such questions slow the operational database to a crawl (much to the annoyance of all the other users) then that interference with the operational database is a problem that needs to be addressed.

2. Questions that span disparate data sources

Imagine your advertising department has its own database that stores information about the advertising promotions that have been run – where the money was spent geographically, how much was spent, which media were used for the promotion etc. The main Order control database stores the information about how many orders have been taken. Again this information is both geographic and historical – all you have to do is to tie the two together and you can answer the question "Which forms of advertising are effective?" The answer could save you a fortune, but you can't seem to extract the data easily in a usable form.

3. Questions that span multiple dimensions

Dimensions in this sense are entities like time, sales people, product sales, regions etc. For example, if you ask to see a chart that displays how much of each product each sales person has sold in a given year, you are essentially asking to see data from two dimensions – people and product. If you ask to see the same information for each of several years, you are asking for three-dimensional data. Add in a requirement to see the data also broken down by region and you are into four dimensions. Actually visualizing this data can be done in a variety of ways, for example:

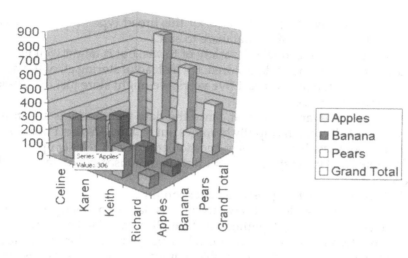

If locating the data and providing an answer to these sorts of questions fills you with horror, or if you know that if anyone asked them, the system would slow to a crawl and users would begin hollering, Business Intelligence tools are for you.

So what is Business Intelligence?

Business Intelligence is IBM's umbrella term for various mechanisms that provide solutions to the types of problem outlined above. There is a whole range of such tools, and we are looking at two of the most commonly used and powerful, namely, Visual Warehouse and the snappily titled DB2 OLAP Server. These two products each provide a basic function.

Visual Warehouse

Visual Warehouse lets you create, manage and automate a data warehouse. OK, so what is a data warehouse?

At its simplest, a data warehouse is an off-line copy of an operational database, usually held on a totally separate machine. Off-line, in this case, means that people are no longer adding to, and altering, the data. Now those large queries that need to examine a large proportion of the records ("How many tins of cat food have we sold in the past five years?") no longer have an impact on users. In addition, since we know that this off-line system is only going to be used for this broad type of query, we can optimize the structure of the database to suit.

This optimization can take a variety of forms, but it might well involve reducing the detail in the data stored. So, instead of storing all of the detail of every sale made over the last five years, we might store just the weekly totals for each product.

The only disadvantage is that, since the data warehouse is an off-line copy, the data it contains rapidly becomes out of date. This isn't usually too important for these broad types of question and we can also set up 'refreshing' systems that bring the data in the data warehouse up to date at regular intervals.

That takes care of the questions that span time.

A data warehouse doesn't have to suck its data from a single source, it can also be used to bring together data from disparate databases, holding it in a central location so that queries can be run against it. This rather neatly takes care of the second class of problem query – those that span disparate data sources. Of course, there is no such thing as a free lunch, as considerable effort is required to ensure that the data is brought together in a compatible form. But if you need the information, it is worth expending the effort.

Visual Warehouse provides you with all the tools you require to set up and maintain a data warehouse. More than that, it provides all sorts of additional features that make automating and controlling the data warehouse easier.

❦ *The descriptions above are clearly both broad and simplistic; if you want more information about data warehousing please read Appendix 1.* ❧

DB2 OLAP Server

DB2 OLAP Server addresses that third class of problem, questions that span multiple dimensions.

❦ *For more detail about the concepts behind OLAP, see Chapter 13.* ❧

If you need the set of benefits from just Visual Warehouse or just those from DB2 OLAP Server, that's fine. It is perfectly possible to use the products independently; however, there is considerable synergy between the two. IBM's experience suggests that people often end up using both for no other reason except that the OLAP side of things can be automated with Visual Warehouse tools.

Terminology

Terminology can become a religious issue, and we refuse to be drawn into the murky waters of the difference between a data 'mart' and a data 'warehouse'.

Data mart often seems to be used to mean a small data warehouse or one that doesn't embrace all of the data within an organization. We think that this sort of distinction is fatally flawed; after all, what is a small amount of data? Ten years ago, a 100 Mbyte database was really impressive; now it isn't. In addition, as we said above, size really isn't important. So, to make our lives easier we'll use the term data warehouse for any off-line database used as described above – regardless of size, location or usage.

We also, with some trepidation, use the terms Column and Field interchangeably. We are aware that Column is the more 'correct' term, but we suspect it is gradually being ousted, rather as the term Relation has mainly been replaced by Table. If we use Column exclusively, we risk looking old fashioned, if we use Field we risk appearing trendy or trivial. Sigh. We've decided upon a liberal, middle of the road approach that will probably end up offending everyone. If it does, our apologies, we really try hard not to tread on anyone's toes.

The "proof of concept" (POC) concept

Some of the people at the IBM Santa Teresa research facility where Business Intelligence tools are developed spend a fair proportion of their time actually helping customers to install and use the software. They advocate a procedure that they call POC, and it works like this.

It is possible to try to calculate the amount of disk space and machine power that will be needed for a data warehouse. Such calculations are likely to be difficult, time consuming, expensive and ultimately yield an equivocal answer. This is not always helpful.

In addition, you can attempt to identify all of the problems within your organization that Business Intelligence could address, and then try to implement a 'Business Intelligence solution' that solves them all. Experience suggests that this will be difficult, not to say almost impossible.

If this sounds like we're saying that you shouldn't launch straight away into a full-blown data warehousing project, that's exactly right. An oft-quoted factoid is that 70% of data warehouse projects fail. They do so for a variety of reasons, but often complexity and time play a major part. Complex systems can take a long time to complete, often several years. If the system does ever actually get up and running, the business requirements are likely to have changed, and nobody is happy with the end result.

POC is much more pragmatic. It says that hardware is now cheap so don't spend too much time doing the sums. Simply buy what seems to be a powerful enough machine and start work. When you start work, don't try to solve all of your problems at once. Instead, try to solve an already identified problem. A well-defined OLAP POC may be, for example, to take an existing hard copy report, identify the data sources needed to generate that report and build an OLAP application to create a live version of it. This gives the users an immediate understanding of the value of Business Intelligence – the importance of such an understanding should not be underestimated. Users are an integral part of any Business Intelligence solution and they, as much as the development team, will feel happier if they can see some immediate benefits.

This 'prototyping' process will have three major benefits. Firstly, as an aid to estimating the size of the final data store, this exercise is a faster and more accurate way of reaching a figure. Secondly, your users may actually get something useful from the new view of this data. A third benefit is that both users and system developers will have gained lots of valuable experience.

This is a strong argument for a quick prototyping project to enable users to see the benefits and for you to gain experience. Once complete, it's likely that it will be easier to make the decision about whether or not to go ahead with a more complex project. It will probably also be easier to justify the expense of super-duper hardware if you can show tangible benefits from the proof of concept work.

Picking a further problem area and developing the warehouse incrementally is a perfectly valid option, giving some control over the complexity and the time scale for the project's development.

What do you need?

One recommendation that we will make (and as forcefully as possible) is that you use a separate box for this prototyping work. It might be possible to install Visual Warehouse and/or DB2 OLAP Server on a machine that's already running an operational database but doing so is likely to affect the performance adversely. As it's likely that performance issues are part of the decision to use Business Intelligence tools, exacerbating the problem won't win you any friends. We strongly advise the purchase of a glitzy new box for the project.

We assume you're using the NT versions, and IBM's recommendation for hardware is a Pentium with 64Mb of RAM as a minimum for the sort of install we demonstrate. We said it in the DB2 for Windows NT book and we'll say it again here – 'Phooey'. This figure should be treated with derision. It's certainly not realistic because it will leave you with a system that's strangled by lack of resources. Below is a screen shot taken from NT which has Visual Warehouse loaded (without any data). As you can see, memory usage is running at nearly 130Mb.

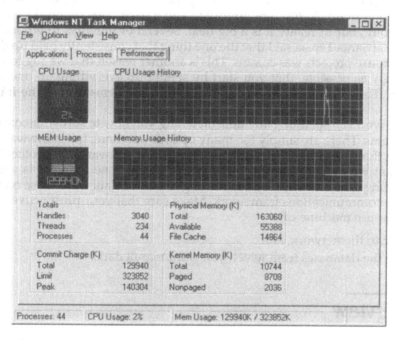

Of course, this figure will vary depending upon configuration, but it makes the point. With memory so cheap (a.k.a. cost effective) buy lots: 256Mb is a good start – work up from there. Have lots of disk space at your disposal too, as warehouses and, more especially, OLAP solutions can chew into it at a great rate.

Kit

Do you have to buy IBM kit? Absolutely not. IBM has long since abandoned its policy of trying to make you buy everything from Big Blue. You run this software on whatever hardware you happen to favor. However, before you ask, we did all of our testing and running on IBM kit. We didn't choose IBM kit because we had to, but because we really do like its machines. They used to be horribly expensive, but now seem very cost-effective, and the build quality, particularly of the portables, is wonderful.

Communications

Before you can get a data warehouse operational, you'll need to make sure that you can do all the communicating you'll need. This sounds like a minor point, but in reality it is a big deal. Several of the guys to whom we spoke at Santa Teresa said that the one thing that consistently held up data warehouse projects was comms. This is another reason that we suggest, as strongly as possible, that you start by setting up everything on one machine. This allows you to ignore the comms. problems during the initial tests.

We won't be spending any time on telling you how to sort your comms. problems. There are simply too many options out there, too many ways of doing things and too wide a range of hardware, software and protocols.

What we can do is point to the whole area as one where it is worth spending time and effort before starting to build a data warehouse on top of the communications framework. Make sure that your prospective data warehouse machine can:

a) talk to the network, and
b) see the databases from which you want to pull data.

Overview

We said above that Business Intelligence enables you to deal with three fundamental classes of problem and that those problems could be characterized as three types of question that managers typically ask:

1. Questions that span time
2. Questions that span disparate data sources
3. Questions that span multiple dimensions

This book shows you how to use IBM's Business Intelligence tools and, as far as we are concerned, the only reason for learning to use those tools is to solve problems.

So, rather than just writing, "do this, now do that" we are going to run you through the steps necessary to solve each of these classes of problem in turn. It just so happens that, by the time you have run through the steps, you will know enough to use the tools effectively (or so we hope). The plan we follow is:

Installing Visual Warehouse

Checking that the installation is correct

Connecting to Visual Warehouse as a Data Warehouse Administrator

Connecting to a source of data (i.e. an existing operational database)

Using Business Views to extract and transform the data from that source and put it in the data warehouse

By this time you will essentially be able to solve problem 1, a point reached by the end of Chapter 3.

Connecting users to the data warehouse

More about the components within Visual Warehouse

Connecting to disparate data sources

Pulling data in and transforming it so that it appears to the user as a cohesive whole

By this stage you will be able to solve problem 2 – end of Chapter 9.

Installing DB2 OLAP Server

Checking that the installation is correct

Connecting to DB2 OLAP Server as a DWA

Installing and inspecting sample files

Building a test cube

Importing data into DB2 OLAP Server

Adding more data to the existing cube

Creating your first cube using raw data

By this stage you will be able to solve problem 3 – end of Chapter 18.

This list isn't a heading-by-heading list of the chapters; for example, there are chapters on Security and DataGuide that we have slipped in along the way. These aren't essential to answer the basic question, but they are vital if you want to explore IBM's Business Intelligence solution to the full.

What next?

We'll take you through a simple example, which we suggest that you follow as closely as possible – using the same names, sample data etc. When you are happy that you have a reasonable idea of what you are doing, you can happily scrap that work, and run a 'proof of concept exercise' on your own data.

So, let's get going.

Chapter 2

Installation

Where to install all the bits

One of the joys of IBM's Business Intelligence software is that it is very adaptable and highly scalable. One of the features that helps to provide this adaptability is that the various components making up Visual Warehouse can be installed in a multitude of different places. You can, for example, install Visual Warehouse itself on one machine, the actual data contained in the data warehouse on another and you can sit at yet a third machine driving the whole system over the network. We applaud this adaptability because it provides you with a flexible solution (Chapter 12 gives more detail about placing these components). However, we are, for now, going to tell you how to construct a system where everything is installed on a single machine. For a start, this fits in with the 'proof of concept' concept outlined earlier. Secondly, it is the easiest installation to do. Thirdly, we cannot possibly outline all of the potential options. Finally, even if you intend to split the system up eventually, you can start in the way we describe. Once you get the system working, you can relax. Then you can try altering one thing – such as moving the data warehouse to another machine. If it doesn't work you know exactly which bit isn't working, so you can concentrate on fixing that one thing. At worst, you can return to the working system and start again.

First steps

The moment arrives to install Visual Warehouse. We presume that you have identified the machine that will become your Visual Warehouse server and that you have administrator rights on it. *Please see the 'Who should you be?' section in the Introduction – there we make recommendations about the users that you need to create and use in order to follow the examples in this book.*

The following need to be in place and working on that machine before you start to install Visual Warehouse:

- Microsoft Windows NT (Workstation or Server 4.0 or later)
- A network card
- A proven connection to a network
- DB2 for Windows NT
- The SAMPLE database that comes with DB2
- DB2 ODBC (Open Database Connectivity Support)

(The book mentioned earlier, 'DB2 for Windows NT – Fast', provides detailed information about the last three.)

Why are we are so definitive about the network card and network connection? Only because we installed DB2, Visual Warehouse etc. multiple times in preparing this book. Only once did we try it on a machine without a network card. ARGHHHH!!!! Please spare yourself the anguish. (Just for the record it can actually be done but it really isn't worth the effort since you will eventually need a network card anyway so you might as well put it in at the beginning.)

Make sure that the ID you are going to use for this install also has SYSADM rights on DB2.

DB2 uses NT to support NetBIOS, TCP/IP and IPX/SPX protocols. As we said above, comms. (or rather a lack of comms.) is often a problem. Details of setting up all the possible comms. alternatives lie outside the scope of this book, so we'll fall back on the ubiquitous cop out that everyone else seems to use: "Please see your network administrator for details."

We are also going to assume that DB2 is set to auto-start. It doesn't have to be, but the assumption saves us from telling you to manually start it every time NT has to be rebooted!

Databases and connectivity

You might hope, with these two hefty programs already installed, now would be the turn of Visual Warehouse.

Well, almost.

Before we get started using the CD-ROM, a couple of definitions may be helpful. In creating a data warehouse you will be sucking data from somewhere (referred to as the Source) and putting it into somewhere else (the Target). Pretty logical names, really.

As well as absorbing those definitions, you also have to do a bit of housekeeping with DB2 before the install: you should create two databases in DB2. These are a target database and a control database. The target database, given the definition above, is clearly the one that will hold the data in the data warehouse itself. The control database stores everything you enter into Visual Warehouse, and this information becomes useful metadata (see below).

In fact, if you choose a certain type of installation, known as Typical: Stand-alone, Visual Warehouse will create the control and target databases for you. (The control database will be called VWCNTRL and the target given the unwieldy name of VWTGTWHS). The reason we do not follow this path here is because we find it more instructive to perform a custom installation. You may well end up with the same result as if we'd used the Typical: Stand-alone installation but you'll have a better understanding of Visual Warehouse's interactions with DB2 and of the components in Visual Warehouse itself. This, we feel, is fair exchange for a few minutes extra work.

Metadata

The term 'metadata' is sometimes used, in referring to relational databases, in a rather narrow sense to mean 'tables that contain data about the structure of this particular relational database.' If you are used to this definition, then the way IBM uses the term 'metadata' to describe what's inside the control database (see below) seems weird. However, more broadly 'metadata' means 'data which describes other data'. Used like this it describes the contents of the control database perfectly.

Metadata within the control database comes in two flavors: technical and business.

Technical metadata describes the data in a data warehouse, including information about the origin of the data, where its target is located etc. Technical metadata also encompasses the rules by which the data is brought into the warehouse, such as whether it is filtered in any way. The term also covers the rules for transforming source data to data required by the target – these are Business Views.

Business metadata is data which is stored so that users can get quick and easy access to the data stored in a warehouse. Business metadata can identify what data is present in the warehouse, where it is, who "owns" the data, how recently it was updated and so on. It is typically made available to users via some sort of GUI so that they can see what is in the data warehouse.

Technical metadata is, in the main, used by IT/MIS staff to manage, extend, automate and maintain the warehouse using Visual Warehouse functionality. Business metadata is used more by end users for access to the data they require, through the medium of a DataGuide information catalog. DataGuide is included with Visual Warehouse and will be covered in Chapter 11.

So, how do you create the control and target databases manually?

Creating the control and target databases

The easiest way to create the new databases is with DB2's Create Database SmartGuide. So, fire up DB2 on the Visual Warehouse server, make sure you are logged in as SYSADM (or, at the very least, an identity that has the power to create databases). Expand the DB2 Control Center view to the Databases level, right click on Databases, Create and New to start the SmartGuide. Run through it twice to create the two databases.

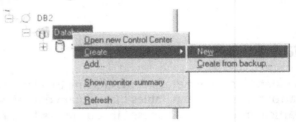

It is worth giving them simple and memorable names like VWCONT (for Visual Warehouse control) and VWTARG (for Visual Warehouse target).

❝ *We've tried to provide a consistent set of examples that work for the steps we outline. If you intend to follow along, it will simplify matters if you use the names for databases, tables etc. that we suggest throughout the book. Anything created will be a learning aid only and therefore disposable, so if the names we use annoy you, don't worry, you'll be rid of them shortly.* ❞

It's also worth keeping things as simple as possible for now and electing the easiest options such as System-Managed Space.

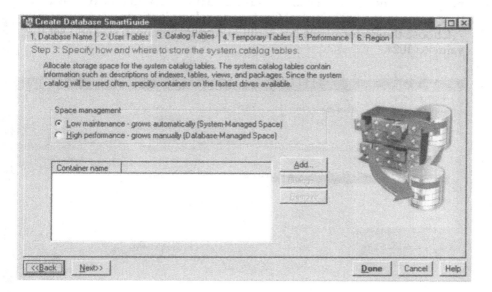

In order to be sure that Visual Warehouse has enough memory to be able to process the SQL commands that it issues, you need to set the application heap size of the control database to 1024. To do this, right click on the database name in the DB2 Control Center and select Configure.

Choose the Performance tab, scroll to Application heap size and set the value to 1024.

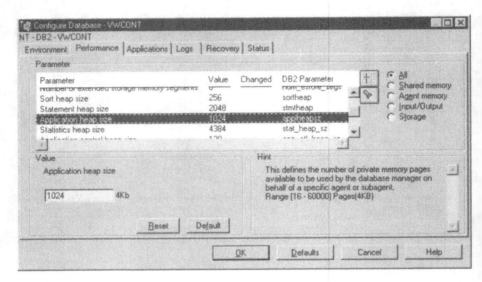

There is no need to create tables within the two databases you've just created, but it is imperative that they are both registered as system DSN (Data Source Name) 32 bit ODBC data sources. This registration is essential to allow Visual Warehouse to connect to the DB2 databases.

From the Windows Control Panel, double click the ODBC icon and in the ODBC Data Source Administrator dialog, choose the System DSN tab. Click the Add button, highlight the IBM DB2 ODBC driver and click Finish.

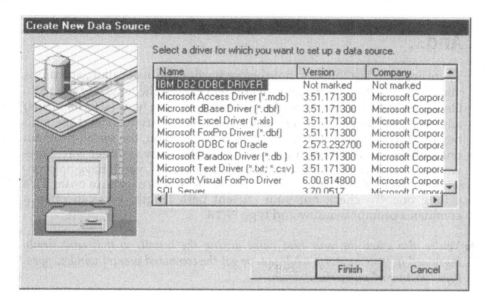

In the Data source name field in the subsequent dialog, select the name of your control database from the pop down list,

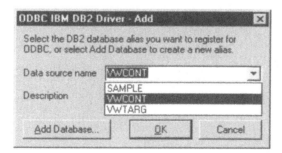

adding a description if you wish. The "Add Database..." button looks particularly tempting at this point, but don't succumb to its lure.

Click the OK button instead. All you're doing here is registering the database for use with a specific connection; as the text in the dialog says (but is so easily overlooked) the Add Database route is for creating a new alias.

Repeat this process for your target database. (If you happen to start again from the Control Panel, be aware that the dialog defaults to the User DSN tab, so check that the System DSN tab is selected before proceeding).

And...

There are a few last things to note before starting the installation, and one is your system path. The install program will extend the length of the path. However, there is a limit to the length that a path can have (450 characters) and there is a danger that the install program will try to extend the path beyond this value. In a rather mean-spirited fashion, the install program only informs you of this danger once installation is well under way. Fore-warned is forearmed. If your path is short and sweet, you'll have no problems, but some shortening (**before** starting the install) may be in order if it's a long one. To check out your current path length, you can open a command prompt window and type PATH.

❝ *You're also asked for your host name during the install, so if it isn't firmly ingrained in your memory, while you've got the command prompt window open, type "hostname" and write it down.* ❞

To check out your path the GUI way, open up the Windows Control Center, double click the System icon, select the Environment tab and find the path system variable.

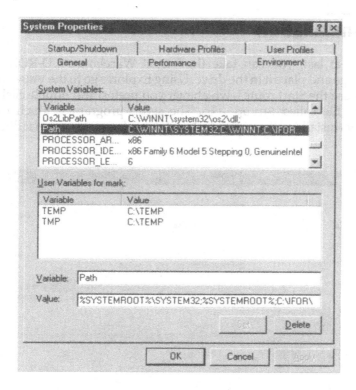

❝ *As an aside, we try always to show the GUI way of doing things, but in this case it seems perverse since the command prompt window is not only faster, but the result is easier to read!* ❞

You can use the GUI to see the host name using Control Panel, Network and inspecting the Identification tab. The entry for Computer Name is, in most cases, the same as the host name.

Finally...

Log on with the Windows NT user ID that meets the specifications described in the introduction (Who should you be?) Close any Windows applications that are running (at the risk of sounding pedantic, this refers to Windows programs, like the DB2 Control Center, but not to Windows services like DB2 – DB2DAS00).

The installation

So now, at last, you can take the Visual Warehouse CD-ROM out of its package and place it in the drive. Using Explorer go to the VWSWIN directory (or use the Start route – whichever you prefer) and double click on (or run) the file called Setup.exe. The setup program is much like any Windows install program and starts with a welcome screen that does what it says.

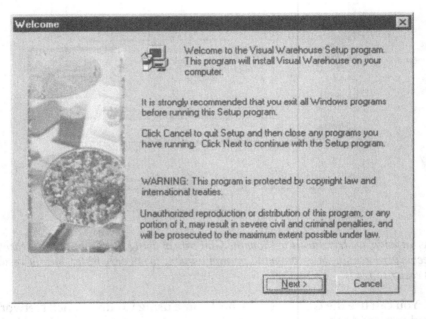

Click Next to continue.

This step allows you to select the type of setup you require. We recommend selecting the Custom install, for reasons outlined earlier.

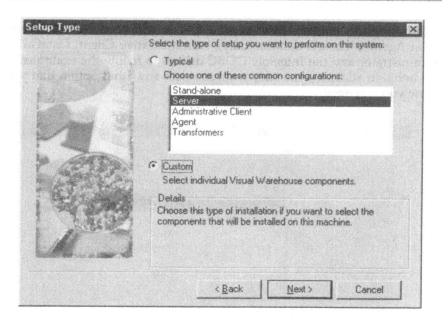

Click next. This step specifies where the Visual Warehouse files are stored. Unless you have reasons for changing them, stick with the defaults for now.

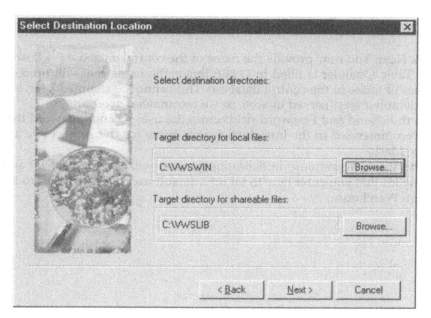

Choosing the components comes next. You will need Server (where-upon Agent is chosen automatically), Administrative Client, DataGuide Administrator and the Intersolv ODBC drivers to follow the examples in this book. In addition, you may want to select any other option that you know you will need.

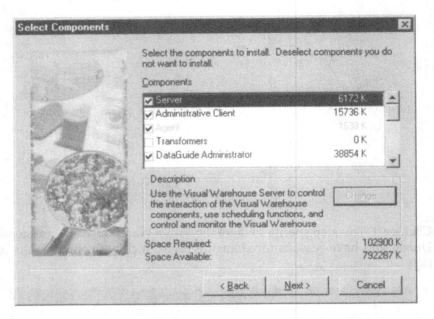

Click Next. You now provide the name of the control database (VWCONT). The Table Qualifier is filled in (IWH): this is the name that will precede names of tables in the control database. This cannot be changed later, but the default always served us well, so we recommend accepting it.

In the Userid and Password fields enter the user ID and password that we recommended in the introduction you create for this project (we are using Mark).

The Visual Warehouse initialization process will use the user ID and password that you enter here to set up a default user ID and password for Visual Warehouse.

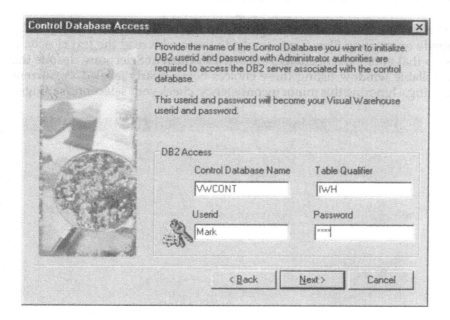

Click Next. The default suggestion for the program folder sounds perfectly sensible, so stick with it.

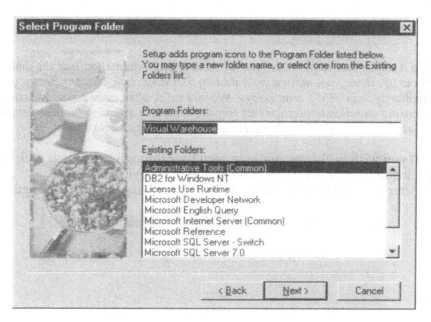

The text indicates that you've given enough information for a start to be made on copying files. Confusingly, to those who read the text closely, it says that your current choices are listed in Current Selections, despite the scrollable window listing these choices being clearly labeled as Current Settings. Ignoring this minor inconsistency, check your selections/settings.

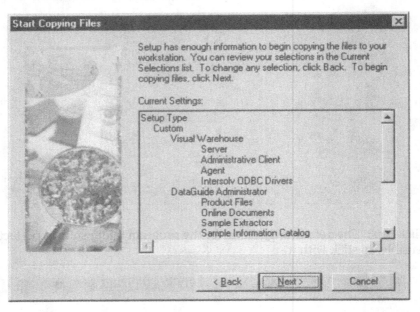

❛ *You'll notice that we're quite keen on reading any information that the dialogs throw up. It may not mean a great deal on first inspection, but it increases your familiarity with IBM's terminology. We find we've often come across something requiring an action or decision that triggers a memory of having "seen something about that a while ago". Such associations can be very valuable.* ❜

If you wish to change anything, step back through the dialogs with the Back button, otherwise click Next to start the copying process.

After some copying, you'll see the warning message about path length,

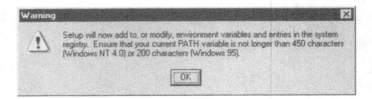

but you can feel smug having dealt with the problem before it arose.

After some more copying and initialization, you should see something like this:

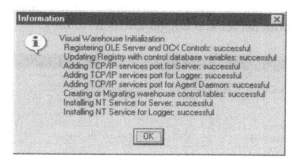

which is encouraging; so click OK and you'll be asked if you want to restart now or later.

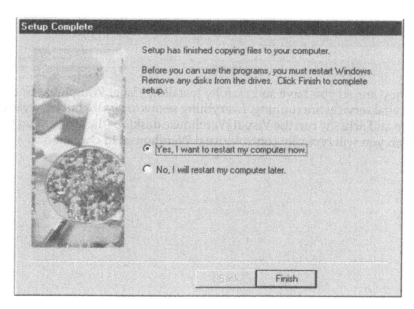

We recommend 'now', so click the Finish button.

Checking that everything is OK

After the restart, from the Services icon in the Control Panel, check that the Visual Warehouse Server and Logger are both running.

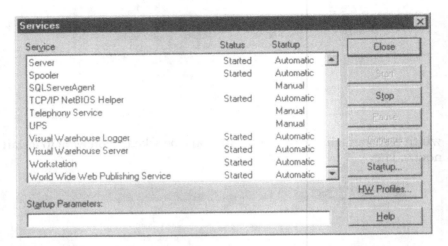

They are, so you have successfully installed Visual Warehouse and the two vital services are running. Everything seems to be OK, but let's wade in there and actually run the Visual Warehouse desktop (the application from which you will typically control Visual Warehouse) to check it out.

From the Windows Start menu, navigate via Programs, Visual Warehouse 5.2 (or whatever version is current when you read this), Visual Warehouse and finally Visual Warehouse desktop. This logon screen appears.

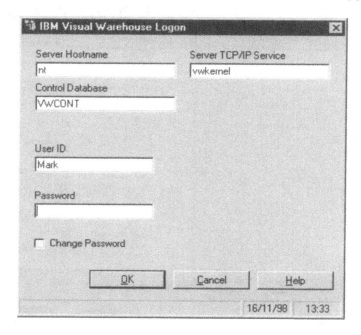

Most of the details should be in place, add anything that is missing. However, check that the case of the user ID is correct. If it isn't, then 'make it so' otherwise the connection will fail. Enter the password (again in the correct case) and press OK.

You'll see a Connecting message on screen briefly, and here's your first view of the Visual Warehouse desktop.

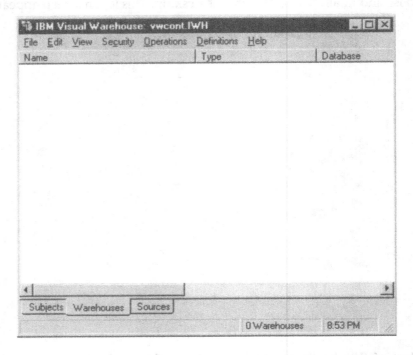

As you can see from the title bar, you are looking at VWCONT.IWH. (During installation, IWH was accepted as the qualifier for tables in the control database). The desktop view has three tabs, unconventionally (and annoyingly) located at the bottom of the window, for moving between the three flavors of desktop, namely Sources, Warehouses and Subjects. Clicking on each tab will show you that there's absolutely nothing in any of them. This is fine, so if you have been able to follow so far then it is likely that Visual Warehouse is properly installed. With any NT application this is a relief, so some degree of relaxing and self-congratulation seems in order.

While the celebrations are in progress, now seems like a good time for a brief recap/overview of what you have achieved.

Recap/overview

You have a nice, new NT box that is destined to become your data warehouse machine. DB2 is running on it and will act as the repository for the data that you are going to put in the data warehouse. More specifically, the data will be stored in a database called VWTARG. DB2 will also hold the metadata for the data warehouse – specifically in a database called VWCONT.

You have just installed Visual Warehouse, and if you look at the two databases from the DB2 Control Center, you'll see that both contain system tables. The control database also contains tables which will hold warehouse metadata, and VWTARG will shortly acquire tables that hold the actual data.

Chapter 3

Creating a data warehouse

Overview of what you are about to do next

Visual Warehouse is now up and running. The next logical step is to populate a data warehouse with some data from a database somewhere.

❝ *The first time we did this, the process seemed rather longwinded.*

- *First you have to create what is called a Source which defines where the data is coming from; in other words, the Source points towards the actual data source.*
- *Then you create another entity called a Warehouse (which isn't a data warehouse, but a repository for the Business Views).*
- *Next you define an entity called a Business View within the Warehouse which defines what data will be pulled into the data warehouse and how it will be altered during that process.*
- *Finally you run the Business View in order to pull the data from the source into the data warehouse. (See Appendix 4 for an overview diagram.)*

This led us to pondering why all of the steps were necessary, and by the time you are halfway through, you may be thinking exactly the same. The answer lies in the adaptability of the system that these steps produce. It seems more sensible to explain that adaptability later, because by then you will have seen all of the bits at least once. So, if for a while, you seem to be pedaling like mad and getting nowhere, take heart. There is method in the madness, and the threads are pulled together at the end of Chapter 9. ❞

You are now at a stage where you can build a small test warehouse. The first step is to define the source of your data (effectively telling Visual Warehouse where to get the data from) and the second is to create the warehouse itself.

Which data source to use?

The next question is what are you going to use as the data source for this first test of the data warehouse? You can, of course, use any reasonable data source that your data warehouse machine can see out there across the network. However, to keep things simple, we're going to use as the data source the copy of DB2 that we know you have running on your data warehouse machine. More specifically, we're going to pull data from the SAMPLE database that comes free with DB2.

At first sight, this may seem a little contrived. Why pull data from a database and put it back into itself? There are several answers. One is that, in fact, we will only be using the same **instance** of DB2 rather than the same database; technically we will be pulling data from the SAMPLE database and it will end up in the VWTARG database. More importantly, we have no idea what other databases you can see from the data warehouse machine, but we know for sure you have DB2 on that machine. So, we'll use it for the first example because it is the only one we know you have. However, if you think of the SAMPLE database as being just another database that could be located anywhere on your network, you have the right idea.

(If you didn't create SAMPLE when you installed DB2, go to the Start menu, Programs, DB2 for Windows NT, First Steps. This opens the First Steps dialog from which you can choose to install SAMPLE.)

Building a test source

IBM uses the term 'Source database' to mean "one from which data is pulled into the data warehouse". IBM also uses the term 'Source' within Visual Warehouse to mean "an entity that points to a Source database and identifies in that source database all of the tables that may be used in the data warehouse." The first thing that you need to build in order to pull data into the data warehouse is a Source.

Assuming that you still have the Visual Warehouse desktop open, click on the Sources tab, and on File, New from the menu. A dialog asks you for the Resource Type – choose DB2 family (because we are about to pull data from a DB2 database)

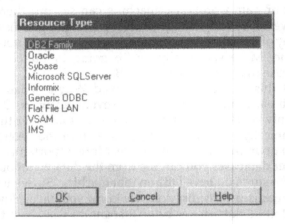

and click on OK.

The next dialog has seven tabs (across the top this time, just to keep you on your toes) starting with General. In the Name field, you fill in a name for the Source you'll be creating. This should reflect the source database to which it will point, so we've used 'DB2 Sample Data'. This field is the only one on this page that it is obligatory to complete. The rest of the fields **can** be ignored since this is a trial of the system, but are very important in an operational system. They are used to hold information that is very useful, not to say essential, for maintenance purposes. One of the main problems with maintaining a data warehouse is knowing where to put, and later find, those snippets of information that are invaluable for future maintenance. One of the great strengths of Visual Warehouse is that it makes this easy. Under Contact you can type in the name of the person responsible for the resource you're accessing. The Location field holds the physical whereabouts of the database server (Room 101, for instance). The Description field holds a brief description that will appear in the desktop view of this resource and so on.

Click on the Agent Sites tab. Here you can stick with the default; the Default Visual Warehouse Agent Site has been entered as a Selected Agent Site. As we're engaged in building a quick sample here, we'll move on to the next tab and leave discussions of Agent Sites (and, indeed, Agents) for the moment.

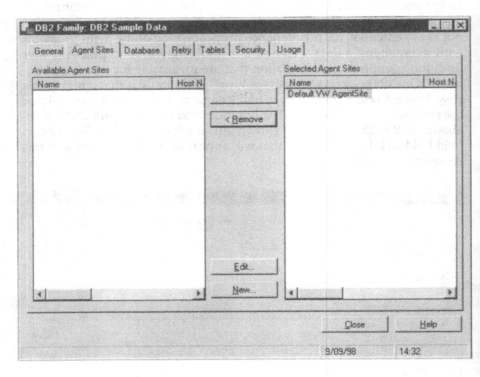

The Database tab requires, in the Database field, the name of the DB2 database to be used as a resource, so enter SAMPLE here. The Type, DB2NT, is already filled in. Now enter a User ID with access to the resource, then type in and verify the password. Finally, enter the System Name (i.e. the host machine name).

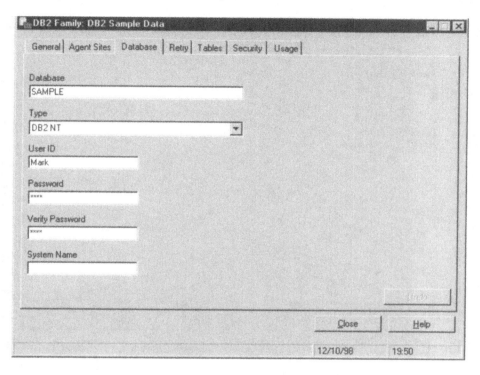

In the Retry tab, you can determine how many times a failed connection should be retried if the connection is not made because of high network traffic. You can set it to retry for a specified number of times at specified time intervals. The default values of three retries at half-hourly intervals is fine for our purposes.

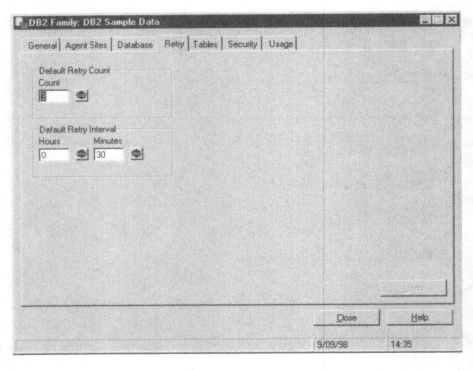

In the Tables tab we get down to the nitty-gritty of defining the tables we want to make available to the data warehouse from, in our case, the SAMPLE database. You can click the New button and enter by hand the information that defines the tables you want, but it is easier to use the Tables... button in the Import panel. If you click on that, this rather bleak dialog box opens.

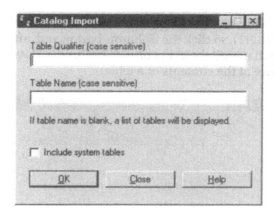

It can be used to filter the list of tables that are about to be presented to you. For example, if we entered MARK as the table qualifier and SALES as the table name, we would only see the table MARK.SALES. For you the qualifier would need to be different (unless you happened to be logged in as MARK when you installed SAMPLE which seems unlikely).

The easiest way to proceed here is simply to enter no information and to click the OK button; this will retrieve a list of all the tables in SAMPLE.

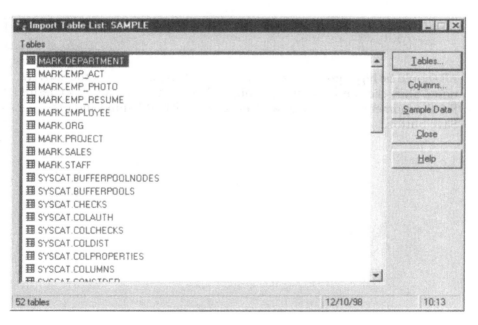

We'll start with the DEPARTMENT table (in our case shown as MARK.DEPARTMENT), so click the Columns button and, after a brief pause, a list of its column names should appear. (The Sample Data button is useful for a quick glance at the contents of a table).

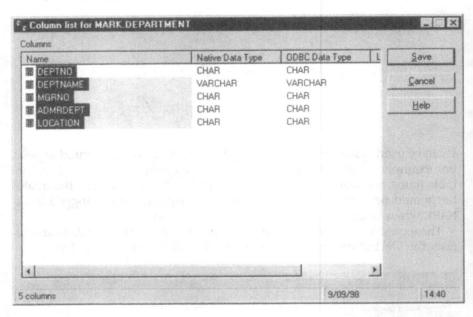

All should be highlighted, and it is possible at this point (using the conventional Shift-click and Ctrl-click) to highlight only a subset if you so desire. For the moment you might as well leave them all highlighted and press the Save button.

Again, after a brief pause, the table name and some details appear in the Tables tab of the Source dialog box. (You might have to move the table list to one side to see this).

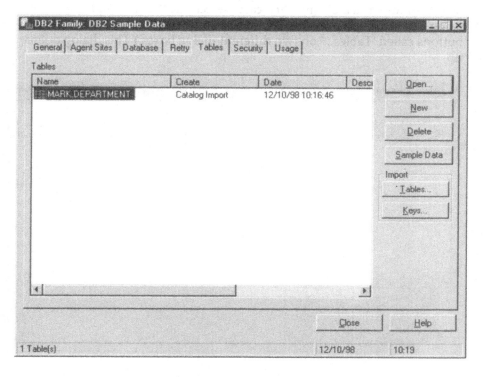

We've just shown you how to import one table, but you can import multiple tables at the same time if you like. The list of available tables should still be open; if not get to it again via the Tables... button. Select multiple tables (in this case select EMPLOYEE and PROJECT using Ctrl-click) and press the Tables... button. (Yes, there are two different buttons called 'Tables...' on two different dialog boxes.) This dialog opens up:

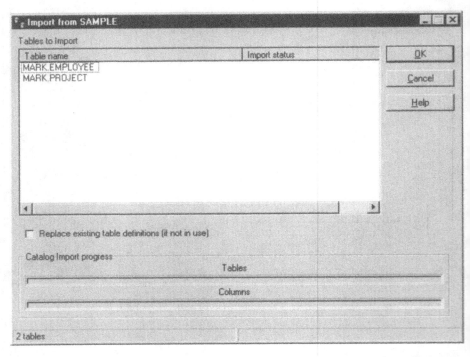

and you can click on the OK button to import them both. After the import has finished, you need to close this dialog box manually. Close the Import Table List too.

OK, so you now have three tables in this Source.

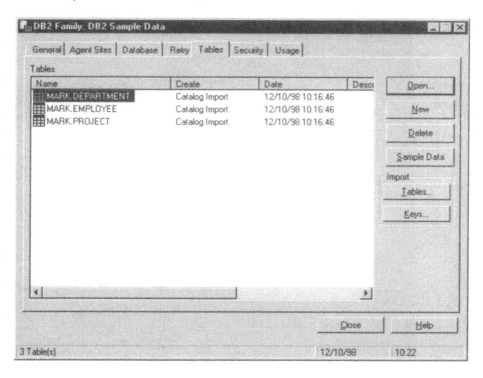

The next step is to tell the source more about these tables – specifically the identity of their primary and foreign keys.

If you double click on DEPARTMENT, a dialog box appears

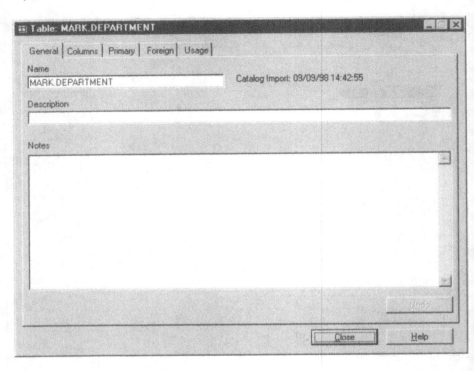

that allows you to edit the properties of this table, at least as it appears in the Source and will appear to the data warehouse. You are **not**, of course, editing the actual structure of the table back in the source database. Note that again (it's a recurrent and excellent theme in Visual Warehouse) you can document what you are doing. At this stage you probably won't bother, but please do in a production system.

There are five tabs in this dialog. Have a browse through all of them just to see what they hold, noting on the way that the Usage tab is empty (we'll come back to it in the Business View section of this chapter). Then turn your attention to Primary. This is where you can identify to the Source the primary key of the table.

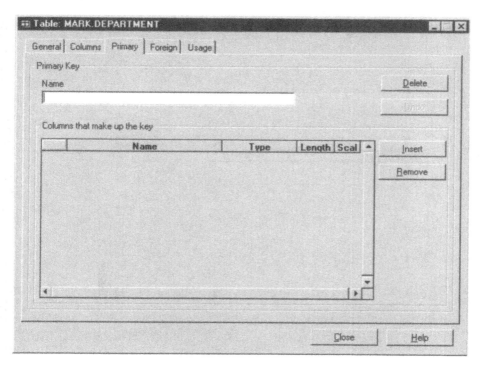

In fact, this information can be automatically imported from DB2 sources using the Keys... button on the dialog box we used earlier.

We'll show you how to do it manually since that process works for all source databases. (In addition, the SAMPLE database is slightly weird in that the supplied tables don't have primary and foreign keys explicitly defined, so the Keys... button won't work for them anyway!) Click on the Insert button, and a field name appears.

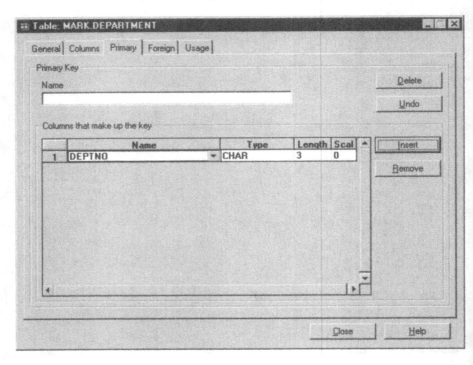

It is DEPTNO, the first field in the table and, because we happen to be familiar with the table, we know that this is a candidate key (that is to say it meets all of the requirements of a primary key). So, DEPTNO is fine and this name can also be used for the name of the primary key that you are required to supply in the upper part of the dialog box.

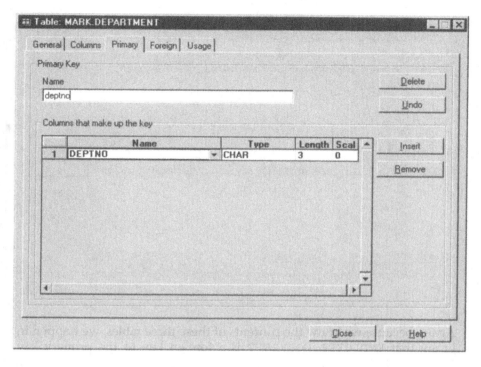

Close this dialog box (an action which accepts the primary key), and define primary keys in a similar way for the other two tables:

PROJECT – PROJNO
EMPLOYEE – EMPNO

Now it is the turn of the foreign keys. Double click on EMPLOYEE again and select the foreign key tab.

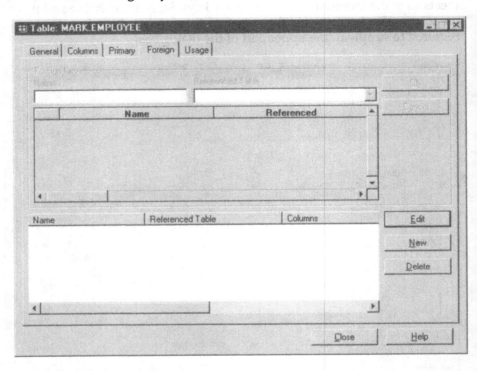

Again, because we know the contents of these three tables, we happen to know that EMPLOYEE.WORKDEPT is a foreign key to the primary key DEPARTMENT.DEPNO.

Click on the New button and nothing seems to change much. But it has, because now in the Foreign Key panel you can pop down the list labeled Referenced Tables and select DEPARTMENT.

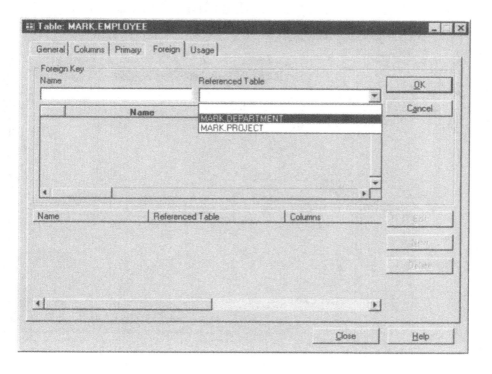

Immediately the dialog box suggests to you that EMPLOYEE . EMPNO might be the foreign key to the primary key in DEPARTMENT.

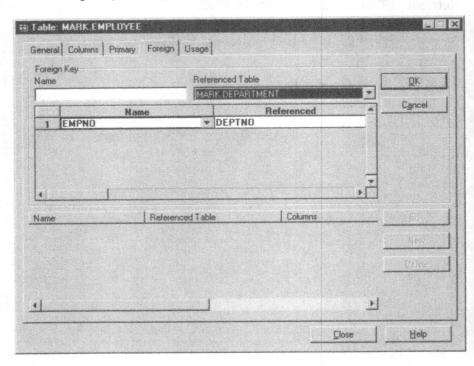

A good try; it just happens to be totally wrong. Never mind, pop down the Name list box and pick the correct option which is WORKDEPT.

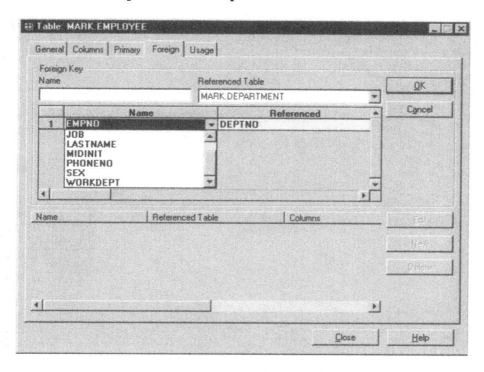

Give the foreign key a name, click on the OK button to accept that foreign key. It is now listed in the lower portion of the screen.

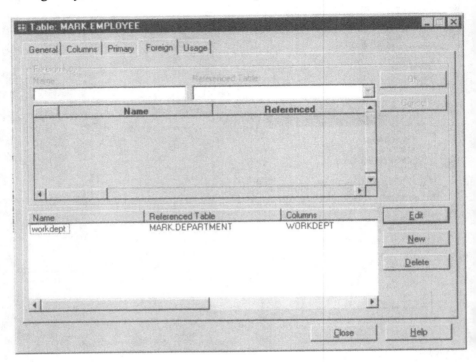

Finally, close the dialog box with the Close button.

Now double click on PROJECT table and define PROJECT.DEPTNO as the foreign key to DEPARTMENT.DEPTNO.

Back in the Source dialog, you can ignore the last two tabs, Security and Usage, accepting the default security and an absence of usage information for now.

With all the tabs visited and completed where necessary, what next? You simply close the Source dialog by clicking on the Close button in whichever tab you find yourself, because your choices and entries have been saved already as you moved between the pages. This leaves us with faintly unsettled feelings; the sense of completing a task by clicking on an OK, Save, Commit or whatever button is missing.

However, back in the Sources desktop, there's DB2 Sample Data as a source, large as life.

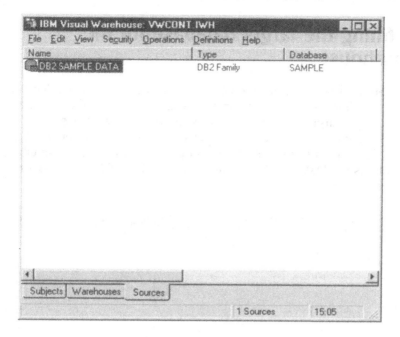

To check or change any of the details just covered, double clicking on the source name will re-open the Sources dialog.

You have successfully set up a Source for your data warehouse. Again, to put this into perspective, despite the fact that IBM uses the term 'import' during this process, you haven't actually imported anything into the data warehouse yet. What you have done is to define, for this particular database (SAMPLE), the tables and fields that **can be** imported into the data warehouse if required.

It might help to think of a Source as a portal through which data can be drawn.

The next step's very easy: you set up a portal through which data can be written to the target database.

Defining the target database for the warehouse

Click on the Warehouses tab on the desktop, and then select File, New. A rather familiar dialog appears, and having just defined a source, the steps to defining a target database for the Warehouse are a breeze.

In the General tab, type in a Target Warehouse Name: ours is SIMPLE TEST. The remaining fields are again optional. In the Database tab, enter VWTARG as the Database Name, along with a User ID and password, and the System Name.

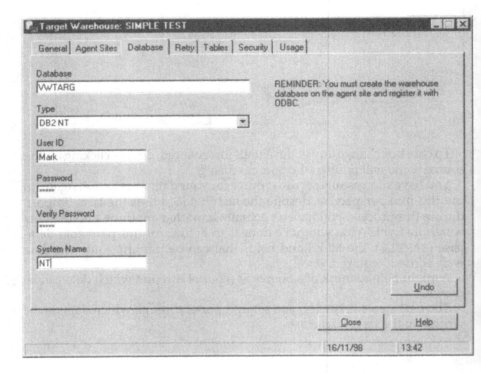

Feel free to browse around the rest of the tabs, but you don't have to define any tables and all of the rest of the defaults should be reasonable, so just select Close when you have seen enough and the new warehouse appears listed in the Warehouses tab.

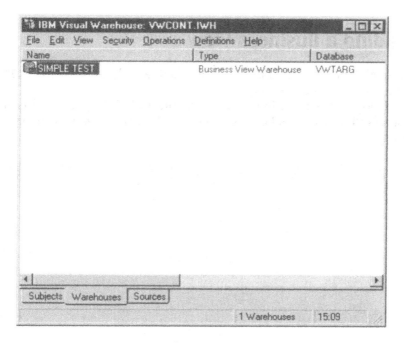

So you've now defined for Visual Warehouse the source from which to import data (SAMPLE) and the target where that data should be placed (VWTARG) – but how do you actually get anything from a to b? The answer is with a Business View.

Business Views

Business View is perhaps one of IBM's less inspired terms. It has overtones of the RDBMS concept of business rules, and of the more general use of the word 'view' to mean a transient virtual vision of data. In fact, in IBM's world, a Business View is something that moves data and, at the same time, can transform it.

Business views are very powerful; they are the tools that move data into the data warehouse and massage it into a state that is useful to your users. A business view can, for example, summarize data, thus enabling users to work with a high level of data abstraction without the overhead of all the detail. Business views can be chained together to perform complex transformations, taking data from various sources and manipulating it into the format that's required in tables that comprise the target database.

Building a Business View

In the Warehouses tab of the desktop, double click on SIMPLE TEST (or highlight it and click File, Open).

A dialog entitled 'Business Views for: SIMPLE TEST' opens: this is the Business View list. Click File, New and you'll see this Create Business View dialog.

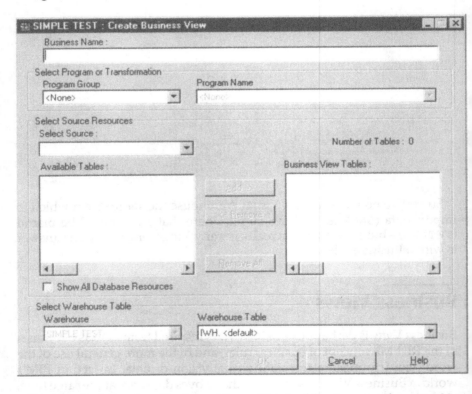

You're asked first for a Business Name. This is obligatory, can be up to 80 characters long and must be unique within Visual Warehouse. Try to choose descriptive names so that the action of the business view is clear to the users. We'll call ours 'Our First Trial Business View'.

❝ *Yes, this does seem a little long, but we have reasons for choosing such a lengthy one.* ❞

From the pop down list called Select Source, choose 'DB2 Sample Data', whereupon the three tables are listed as available.

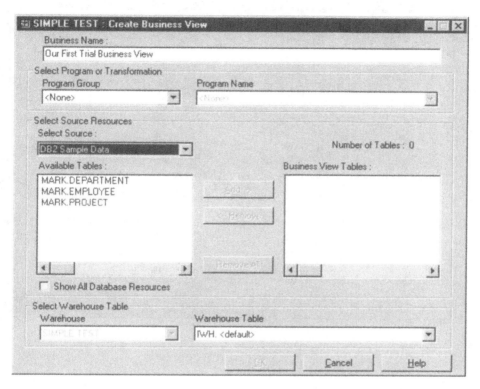

Highlight the table names and click Add to move them to the Business View Tables column (or double click on them). Click OK. This step has determined the tables that the business view will use. When you are building a real system you are, of course, free to choose any number of tables, you don't have to use all of them.

The subsequent six-tabbed dialog is where you define what the business view will actually do. From the first tab, Column Mapping, you decide which columns from the source tables you wish to appear in the warehouse table.

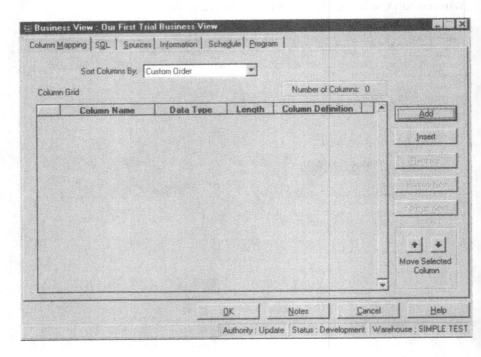

Click on the Add button to see a list of the fields in one of the tables. In the case of the screen shot it is MARK.DEPARTMENT.

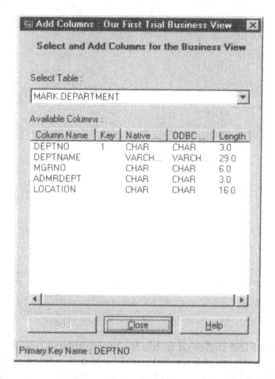

We'll take DEPTNAME and LOCATION, so highlight them and click Add (or just double click each in turn). Then select the table EMPLOYEE and add FIRSTNME, LASTNAME, SEX and SALARY. Finally, from PROJECT select and add PROJNAME.

Close the selection dialog for a clear view of the fields you've chosen.

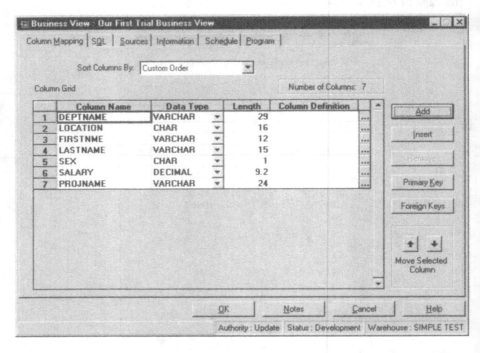

You can change the order of fields by highlighting one and clicking the up or down arrow in the Move Selected Column button panel. Using the Sort Columns By selection is another way of changing the column order; the help system outlines the five different sort types. (Click Help and follow the hyperlinks to Column Mapping and Sort Columns By).

Notes to describe the business view more fully can be added by clicking the Notes button at the bottom of the dialog.

Now look at the SQL tab; it shows you the three tables, complete with the primary keys (defined when you created the Source) highlighted in blue. You need to show Visual Warehouse the joins that you want it to use between the tables. So, click on DEPARTMENT.DEPTNO, then on EMPLOYEE.WORKDEPT and finally on the Join button. A line should appear as shown.

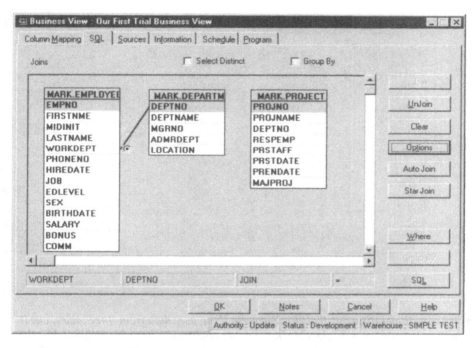

❧ *These screen shots are taken from Visual Warehouse version 3.1 simply because, at the time of writing, certain features of this part of the interface weren't fully implemented in the beta of 5.2 that we used. This shouldn't be a problem because the changes to the design of the interface are minimal. The only major difference seems to be that the 5.2 version of this window has gained a rather useful 'Test SQL' button which does just what the name suggests!* ❧

You can use the Auto Join to make the correct join between PROJECT and DEPARTMENT because Auto Join will join fields of the same name and compatible data types.

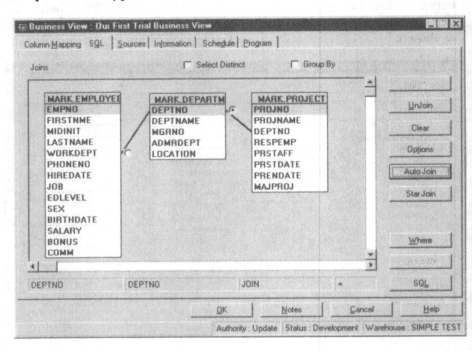

❡ *It is worth pointing out that this Business View uses data from three tables, but it will only generate a single table in the data warehouse. That table is defined by the choices you have just made with these two tabs, and is summarized in the SQL statement shown below. This behavior is mandatory – by that we mean that any Business View can only ever generate a single table in the data warehouse. Indeed, if you think of a Business View as a schedulable SQL statement that always generates a table, you will have a good general view of what a Business View is and how it works.* ❡

You can see the SQL that will be used by the Business View to extract the data and place it into the data warehouse by clicking on the SQL button – you'll be asked if you want to save the business view when you make this click, so reply Yes.

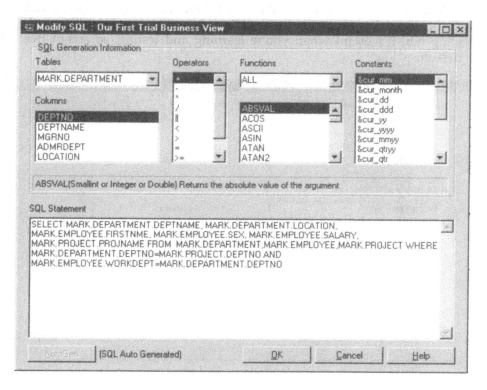

It may well be clear that here is where a great deal of the power of the Business View lies. You can hand-craft the SQL necessary to extract just the data you want. Here we are performing a trivial data extraction, just to show you where all the bits are located. Once you are happy that you have a good overview, this is one area of Visual Warehouse that will repay much more detailed investigation.

Click OK to leave the Modify SQL window and have a look at the other tabs. All are full of interesting possibilities, but the only one we will use for now is the Schedule tab. This allows you to schedule when the Business View will run. For now, make sure that the 'Allow Populate By Request' option is checked, which it should be by default. This will allow you to run the business view at any time, over-riding any settings made in this scheduling tab. It's useful when you're learning and testing, so accept this default.

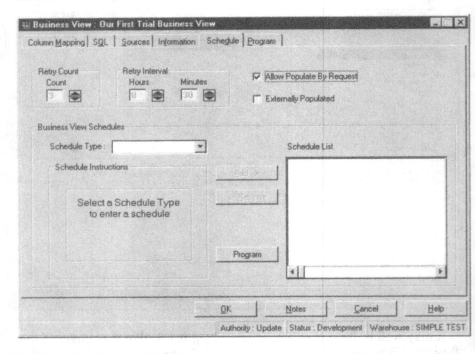

Finally, click OK to finish.

Back in the Business Views list, the new business view is shown.

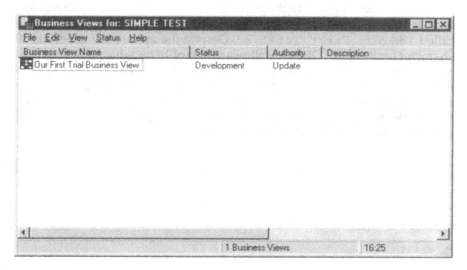

Just to double check all is well, close the Business Views list, return to the Warehouses desktop and highlight SIMPLE TEST on the Warehouses tab, click File, Properties. Under the Tables tab, you should see a new table called IWH.Our_First_Trial_Bu. Despite the apparently generous 80 character limit earlier, DB2 only allows a limit of 18 for table names so truncation can occur at this point. This means that we, in practice, tend to keep Business View names to 18 characters or fewer just to ensure that the names always marry up. If you need or want longer names in your production implementation, you can, of course, use them, but for a trial run like ours, they are an unnecessary complication.

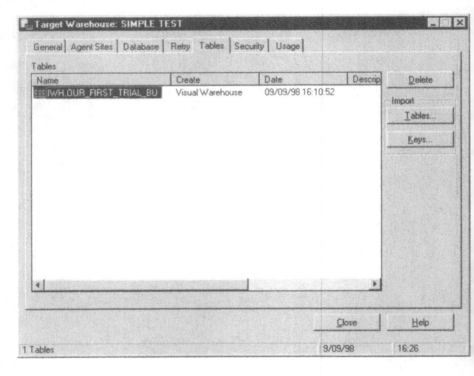

If you click on the Usage tab, you should see that this Warehouse is going to be used by the Business View that you have just created.

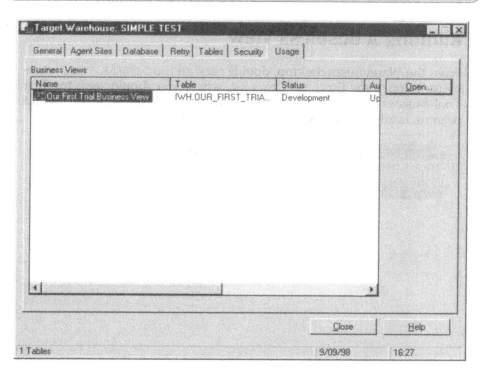

Now you have all the necessary components, and it only remains to run the Business View so that it will carry out its task.

Running a Business View

From the Warehouses desktop, double click on the SIMPLE TEST warehouse to open the Business Views list, where you should see 'Our First Trial Business View'; highlight it by clicking on it once. In the second column, headed Status, is the word 'Development'.

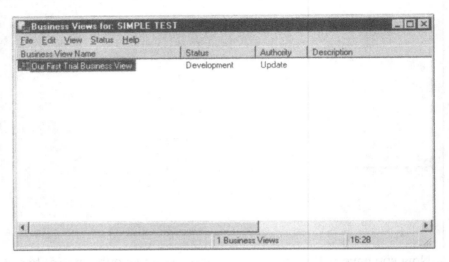

We'll check out the status property later; for now simply click on Status in the menu and click on the first entry, Promote to Test. After a brief pause the status should update.

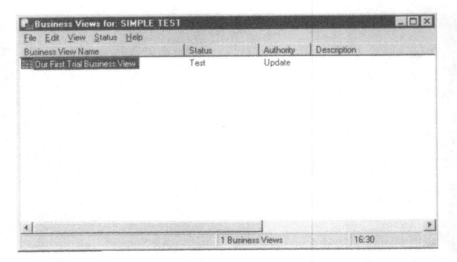

To run the newly-promoted business view, return to the Warehouses desktop and select Operations, Work in Progress.
You may see this message:

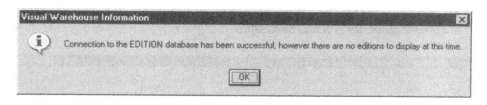

just click OK to continue (Editions are covered later on in Chapter 6).

This window displays an entry for each Business View that has been carried out and tells you whether there have been any problems with running it. None appear as yet because you haven't run any.

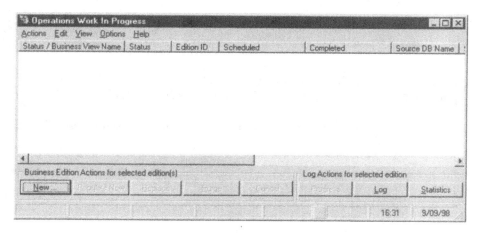

❧ *The full title of the Work in Progress window (as if that wasn't long enough) is the Operations Work in Progress window. Not surprisingly it's often shortened to the WIP window.* ❧

To run 'Our First Trial Business View' manually, click on the New button at the bottom, highlight it and click OK (or double click on 'Our First Trial Business View'). Keep an eye on the Work in Progress window; you should see 'Our First Trial Business View' appearing with the word 'Populating' in the status column – this means the table is being created in the target database and filled with data. When the business view has completed, it will appear in this list looking like the screen shot below, with the magic word 'Successful' in the status column.

❝ *Confusingly, the word 'status' is used in two ways to describe Business Views.*

- *Each view has a status to describe its progress towards completion – you've just changed your first view's status from Development to Test.*
- *Once a view has been run, it also has a status to describe how it performed; in the example above, the run was Successful.* ❞

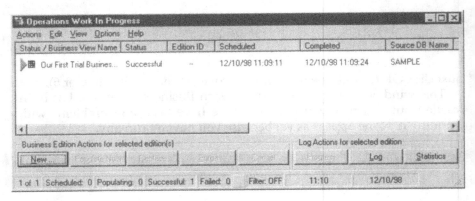

If you duck out to DB2 and look at the list of tables in the VWTARG database, you'll see that Our_First_Trial_Bu now exists as a table.

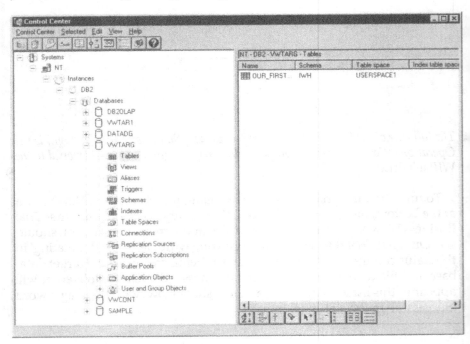

❝ *To make things clearer in this screenshot, we've set a filter in the DB2 Control Center to hide the system tables.* ❞

This table is a static, non-normalized, snapshot of a subset of the data that was in those three tables at the moment the Business View was run.

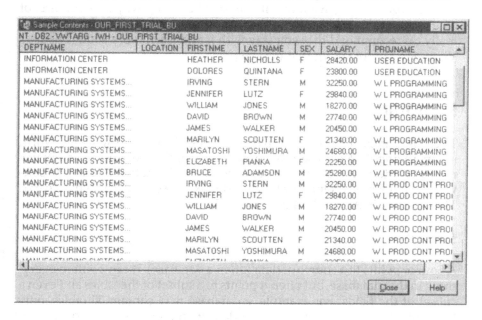

DEPTNAME	LOCATION	FIRSTNME	LASTNAME	SEX	SALARY	PROJNAME
INFORMATION CENTER		HEATHER	NICHOLLS	F	28420.00	USER EDUCATION
INFORMATION CENTER		DOLORES	QUINTANA	F	23800.00	USER EDUCATION
MANUFACTURING SYSTEMS...		IRVING	STERN	M	32250.00	W L PROGRAMMING
MANUFACTURING SYSTEMS...		JENNIFER	LUTZ	F	29840.00	W L PROGRAMMING
MANUFACTURING SYSTEMS...		WILLIAM	JONES	M	18270.00	W L PROGRAMMING
MANUFACTURING SYSTEMS...		DAVID	BROWN	M	27740.00	W L PROGRAMMING
MANUFACTURING SYSTEMS...		JAMES	WALKER	M	20450.00	W L PROGRAMMING
MANUFACTURING SYSTEMS...		MARILYN	SCOUTTEN	F	21340.00	W L PROGRAMMING
MANUFACTURING SYSTEMS...		MASATOSHI	YOSHIMURA	M	24680.00	W L PROGRAMMING
MANUFACTURING SYSTEMS...		ELIZABETH	PIANKA	F	22250.00	W L PROGRAMMING
MANUFACTURING SYSTEMS...		BRUCE	ADAMSON	M	25280.00	W L PROGRAMMING
MANUFACTURING SYSTEMS...		IRVING	STERN	M	32250.00	W L PROD CONT PROI
MANUFACTURING SYSTEMS...		JENNIFER	LUTZ	F	29840.00	W L PROD CONT PROI
MANUFACTURING SYSTEMS...		WILLIAM	JONES	M	18270.00	W L PROD CONT PROI
MANUFACTURING SYSTEMS...		DAVID	BROWN	M	27740.00	W L PROD CONT PROI
MANUFACTURING SYSTEMS...		JAMES	WALKER	M	20450.00	W L PROD CONT PROI
MANUFACTURING SYSTEMS...		MARILYN	SCOUTTEN	F	21340.00	W L PROD CONT PROI
MANUFACTURING SYSTEMS...		MASATOSHI	YOSHIMURA	M	24680.00	W L PROD CONT PROI

❝ *Yes, the data is de-normalized. We don't intend to tell you how to structure data warehouses in general, but, because normalization is often seen as a religious issue, it is worth pointing out that the data in a data warehouse is often de-normalized. This is normal (if you'll pardon the expression) and nothing to be ashamed of.* ❞

Yo! You've reached an important milestone (kilometer post?). You can allow your users (specifically those managers who need to run complex queries) access to this table while the other tables continue to be updated by other users of the database. To keep the 'managers' table' up to date you can run the Business View every night, every week, every month, whatever, using the scheduler (and we show you how to do this in Chapter 5).

Solving problem one

We said in the introduction that Business Intelligence could be used to solve three sorts of problem. You now know the essentials necessary to solve the first problem – how to make data available to managers so that they can run large queries without totally socking the performance of the operational system.

In truth, you are very close to solving the second problem (pulling together data from disparate sources) but we intend leaving the details until Chapter 9. Yes, we know it sounds like a long way and you are, of course, free to leap instantly to that chapter to see how it is done. But we really do recommend that you stay with it and learn more about Business Views etc. before taking that next step.

Summary

There is a great deal of information to absorb here, so it seems worth summarizing it. We'll use less formal, more anthropomorphic language, not in an attempt to infuriate purists (who usually hate references to software as if it was sentient) but to try and make the overall concepts clearer. The diagram in Appendix 4 may also help.

Source

A Source points to a source of data (often a database). It **can** point to everything in that database, but often it points to a subset of the tables and even a subset of the fields. For example, a database may contain 50 tables, only three of which are relevant to the data warehouse, so the Source will simply point to those three.

Note that one Source may only ever point to one source of data, never more.

Think of a Source as a guy whose sole job is to point out the 'useful' data in one of the sources of data that exist within your organization. Does the Source know about any of the other possible sources? No. Does it know the final destination of the data to which it points (in other words, does it know where in the data warehouse the data will fit)? No. And it probably doesn't care – it just lives to point (so you can never accuse a Source of being pointless).

Another way of thinking about a Source is as a service provider; its customers are Business Views. Note that multiple Business Views can use the services of a single Source.

Business View

A Business View can be thought of, in many ways, as a pre-stored query that can be scheduled to run at regular intervals.

Just like a query, the result of running a Business View can only ever be one (and never more than one) table. That table is stored in a DB2 database and makes up one of the tables in a data warehouse. A Business View can pull data from one (never more than one) Source.

So you can think of each Business View as a link between one Source and one table in a data warehouse.

Warehouse

A Warehouse (note that we aren't talking about a data warehouse at this point) is simply collection of Business Views. A warehouse itself also points to one (never more) DB2 database wherein the data warehouse is stored. It follows therefore that each Business View contained within a given Warehouse can point only to the same single target DB2 database.

What do you do next?

We strongly recommend that you spend some time playing with the elements we've introduced in this chapter. Run through this set of operations several times creating more Sources, Warehouses and Business Views. This will help you to get a feel for all of the bits and how they work together.

In fact, in order to follow along with the steps in Chapter 5, you will need to create three business views called 'Foo', 'Baa' and 'Penguin'. Building them will consolidate what you've learned, so we suggest you do that now. These Business Views are very simple and all use DB2 SAMPLE DATA as their data source. 'Foo' simply pulls in all the fields in the EMPLOYEE table, 'Baa' does the same with PROJECT, and 'Penguin' with DEPARTMENT.

You must also set the primary keys for each of these views; these are EMPNO, PROJNO and DEPTNO respectively. To do this, click the Primary Key button in the Column Mapping dialog and click Insert in the resulting window. A likely candidate is offered; if it's the right one all you have to do is add a name for the primary key. Often the field name is a reasonable choice. Click OK to complete the process.

If you should happen to forget to identify the primary key when you create a business view, you can return and do it later. It's best done with the view in Development status, but you can do it when the view is in Test status. If you do, the status will read 'Test (Add column/keys pending)' and you should click on Status and choose the newly-arrived Add New Column/Keys option. After this, the message disappears and the status returns to simply 'Test'.

As you'll have noticed along the way, there are all manner of tweaks and extras in all of those dialog boxes that we skipped delicately over. You don't need to know every possible option in these, but some of them are very useful when construction of your data warehouse begins in earnest. So Chapters 5, 6 and 7 essentially run over the same ground as this chapter but give you more detail about the processes that we think you will find useful.

Chapter 4

Making a connection to the data warehouse

Making a connection to the data warehouse

The whole point of setting up a data warehouse is to allow users to get at the data you have placed in there. Ultimately, once you have built a production system, Visual Warehouse will be populating the data warehouse at regular intervals, and your users will be using some kind of front-end to log on to DB2 and to browse through the data. The choice of front-end is, of course, entirely up to you and your users.

We are assuming that you and your users already have some way of connecting to your current operational databases which may or may not include DB2. Clearly, since the data warehouse is stored in DB2, you (both you personally and your users) will need to be able to connect to DB2 via some front-end tool or other.

In our book on DB2 we cover the mechanics of making such a connection from five different front-ends:

- Access
- Approach
- Delphi
- Visual Basic
- Java

It seems pointless to go over the same ground again in this book because if we keep on putting DB2 specific (rather than data warehouse specific) information in here, the book just keeps on growing. However, we have put on the CD-ROM a set of code examples for each of the above front-ends which comes originally from the DB2 book (see Appendix 3). These examples (and the associated READMEs) should help you to set up an initial connection to DB2. As in the DB2 book we provide no guarantee that they will work in your particular environment, but they were tested reasonably thoroughly before shipping with the last book and we haven't had any complaints so far!

Whatever front-end you intend to provide for your users, it is worth at this point making sure that you personally, as the DWA (Data Warehouse Administrator), can connect to DB2 via a front end – for two reasons.

- It's fun.
- Such a connection enables you to connect to the source data (in SAMPLE) and the data warehouse at the same time.

In turn, this enables you to perform checks on your work as you go. For example, you will almost certainly want to alter the source data, re-populate the data warehouse and check that the change really has appeared where you expected. (Not, of course, that we are suggesting that you would ever actually make a mistake; after all, we never make them ourselves....)

Here, for example, we are using Access to connect to both SAMPLE and VWTARG. On top of Access, we have a window open in which the Visual Warehouse desktop is running.

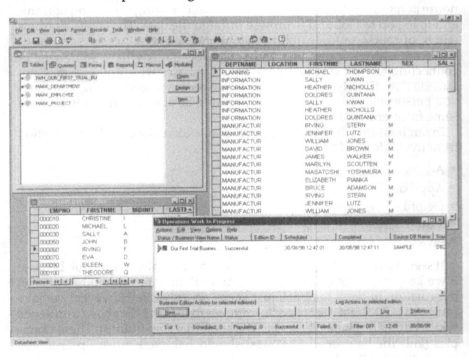

If we change Sally's name to SALLYXXXX (rather a cruel move, but we're sure she'll get used to it) in the EMPLOYEE table, repopulate the data warehouse and then refresh the Access view of the data warehouse table, lo and behold, Sally's name has, indeed, altered in the data warehouse.

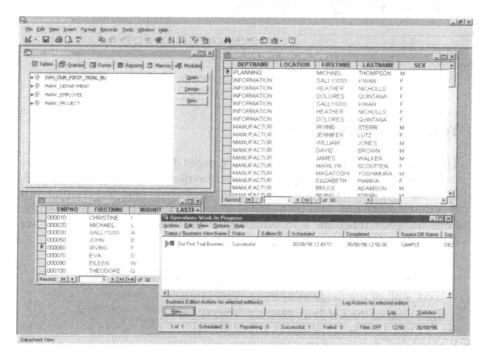

This sort of connection, all within two windows, all running on the same machine, is invaluable for testing your work.

Chapter 5

Business Views

Your starting point

This chapter assumes that you have created the three Business Views called 'Foo', 'Baa' and 'Penguin' that are described at the end of Chapter 3. Obviously you don't have to create these in order to read this chapter, but it is much more fun (and instructive) to follow the steps that we describe here on your machine – in which case the three Business Views are essential.

For reference:

'Penguin' shows all of the fields in SAMPLE.DEPARTMENT
'Foo' – all of the fields in SAMPLE.EMPLOYEE
'Baa' – all of the fields in SAMPLE.PROJECT

❢ *We haven't chosen these names for silliness' sake, but for ease of identification. If we called them things like 'Dept' or 'Project', they would share names with other components (such as tables) and we would have to identify the object type constantly. This way, if you see a reference to 'Foo', you know instantly that we mean a Business View, and you can concentrate on how to use them without wasting time on identification.*

Just for interest, Foo and Baa are 'metasyntactic variables', a delightful term which simply means 'a sample name for absolutely anything'. Baa can also be spelled bar, so perhaps our choice indicate that we feel a bit sheepish about using metasyntactic variables... ❢

Business Views

By now it ought to be clear that Business Views are the guys that do all of the real work in Visual Warehouse in the sense that a Business View actually controls how the data is moved into the data warehouse, so it is worth spending some time getting to know them better.

Status

Business Views are extremely status conscious (just like people). Unlike humans, Business Views have a very rigorously defined status system. A Business View must be in one of three possible status states:

- Development
- Test
- Production

❝ *'Status states' sounds so sibilantly similar to a stutter or stammer that we'll simply call them states.* ❞

You will find that you can only perform certain operations on a Business View when it is in a particular state. For example, you can't change the scheduling of a Business View when it is in Production status. So, let's have a look at the different states.

We'll work on the Business View called 'Penguin' for this demonstration. From the Visual Warehouse desktop, double click on SIMPLE TEST and single click on 'Penguin' to highlight it. Then use the Status menu option to change the Status as required.

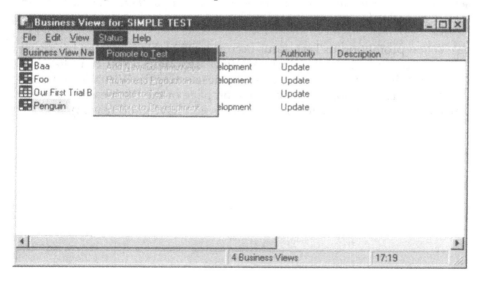

Development status

A Business View in Development status has an icon looking rather like a mostly blue Rubik's Cube (remember those?)

As you might guess, Development is the lowest status and it's the one in which all Business Views start. You're free to define and edit the definition in the Business View notebook. At this stage the Business View alone has been created: the table in which the data will be stored does not yet exist. As a consequence, you cannot populate the table by running the Business View – first you must promote it to Test status.

Test status

The icon for a Business View with Test status looks like a mainly yellow Rubik's Cube.

❟ *It's a shame we can't use color for these icons – they all look more or less the same in black-and-white!* ❜

When promotion to Test status occurs, a DB2 table is created by Visual Warehouse based on the Business View definition. (You can alter this default behavior if you really want to by deselecting the 'Visual Warehouse Created Table' option in the information page of the Business View notebook, but our advice is don't do so unless you have good reason).

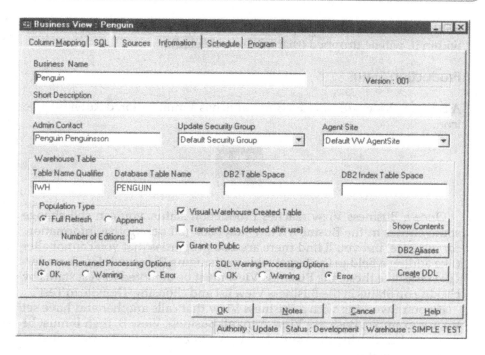

Incidentally, it is here in the Information page that you can, if you so desire, alter the default Table name. This is another way around the generation of unfortunate names like 'OUR_FIRST_TRIAL_BU' that was discussed in Chapter 3.

One aspect of both Development and Test status that is worth stressing (this is code for 'it caught us out the first time around') is that the schedule tab is active; that is, it allows you to schedule the Business View to run at some time in the future. However, it is a rule that only Business Views in Production status have active schedules – so you can schedule away to your heart's content in the other two states but the Business View won't run at the allotted time unless you promote it to Production status. You can, however, run it **manually** from the Work in Progress window if it is in Test status or above, as we did earlier. (See below for more information about scheduling).

If you're working with Business Views that call other Business Views (again, this process is discussed in detail below), it is worth knowing that Test status Business Views can call other Business Views with Development or Test status, but not Production status ones.

When a Business View has been tested and found to behave as required, it can be promoted to Production status. If testing did not prove satisfactory, the Business View can be demoted to Development status. When you do this, any table it has generated in the target warehouse, and the data within it, will be dropped (that is to say, deleted).

Production Status

A Business View with Production status has a multi-colored Rubik's Cube icon.

Once a Business View reaches Production status, you can still change some entries in the Business View notebook (all descriptive information, for instance) but you'll find there are also properties that you cannot alter (like adding a field to the target table or changing the schedule). To undertake tasks like these, the Business View must be demoted to Test status by clicking on Status in the Business View list and choosing 'Demote to Test'.

If you're working with a Business View that calls another and have set up, for example, Business View A to call Business View B, then B must be promoted to Production status before A can be successfully promoted to Production status.

Status summary

The bottom line is that all Business Views have a status. They start as Development, move to Test (for testing purposes) and finally, when they are ready for production use, move to Production status. Simple, really. You also need to remember that Visual Warehouse only allows certain actions to be performed on a Business View when it has the correct status. So, if you are trying to alter some property of a Business View and Visual Warehouse refuses to let you do it, you probably need to change the status.

Deleting your work

We have been encouraging you to play around creating more Business Views. This is good, so please continue to experiment. However, at some stage you will want to put aside childish things (in other words, ditch these test systems). The following rules apply:

- Business Views have to be demoted to Development status before they can be deleted.
- All Business Views have to be removed from a Warehouse before it can be deleted.
- Sources cannot be deleted until the Warehouses that use them are removed.

These rules are accurate, but a little unhelpful when expressed in this rather blunt way. Buried in these rules is the information that the correct order for deletion is:

- Demote the relevant Business Views to Development status and delete them.
- When all of the Business Views in a Warehouse have been deleted, the Warehouse can be deleted.
- When all of the Warehouses that use a Source have been deleted, that Source can be deleted.

You should also be aware that if primary/foreign keys are set up, the child tables (those with foreign keys) must be deleted before the parent tables (those with primary keys).

Scheduling – why schedule?

The obvious answer is that Business Views run against operational databases and can have a potentially detrimental effect on the performance of those databases. Scheduling allows you to run the Business View at the best possible time (usually at night or over a weekend). More importantly, the ability to schedule jobs means that you can be sleeping the sleep of the well-prepared while the data is sucked into the data warehouse.

Scheduling falls into two main categories.

Firstly, you can schedule a given Business View to run at any time interval you choose.

They can be scheduled to run at 1:00 AM every morning, or at the end of each week, or once a minute (**don't** do this on a real live system!) or any possible time period you choose. The data that's needed to satisfy the Finance department (if anything ever **can** satisfy a Finance department) can be ready and waiting every Wednesday morning, or alternate Wednesday mornings – whatever. For the sake of any other name, we can call this 'Time-based' Scheduling.

Secondly, you can schedule Business Views so that they are mutually interdependent; so, for example, you can set up a Business View which will only run after another Business View has successfully finished running.

Why would you want to do this? There are many reasons, but here is one. Suppose that your company has four sales databases located in four different locations – one in the North of the country, one in the East and so on. You have four Business Views called North, East, South and West that run once a week and create four tables in the data warehouse that summarize the sales in each region. Once those Business Views have run, you want to run another (called Overview) which uses the information in those four tables to produce a table that summarizes the overall sales for the entire company. Clearly it is essential that the last Business View doesn't run until the first four have completed. We'll call this 'Cascade' scheduling.

Time-based scheduling

From the Warehouses desktop, double click on the SIMPLE TEST warehouse. Make sure that 'Penguin' is in Test status and then double click it. When the dialog opens, click on the Schedule tab.

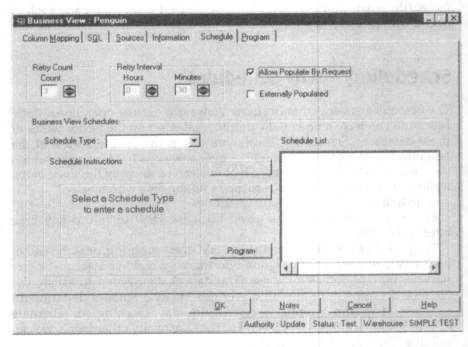

The lower two-thirds of the page is headed Business View Schedules. Pop down the list of schedule types. There are sixteen of these, and different controls appear in the Schedule Instructions panel for each one. Daily lets you specify the time in hours and minutes, Weekly the time and the day, Monthly the time and the day of the month, and so on.

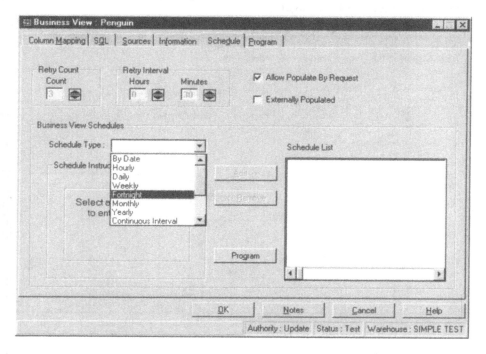

Take some time to have a look at the first eight options (we'll cover the rest later). Curiously when you're setting the time you cannot simply type in a number of hours or minutes but must use the arrowhead buttons.

When your schedule is complete, click Add to place it in the Schedule List on the right. If you decide it isn't correct, highlight it and click the Remove button, and start again.

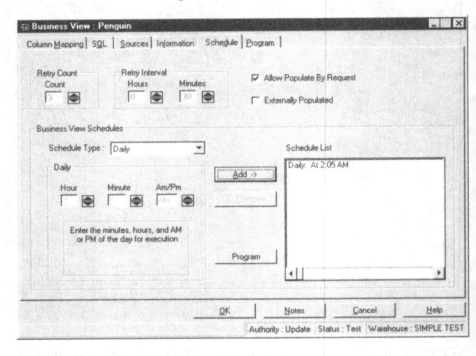

You can choose several different options to provide the exact schedule that you need.

Now schedule this Business View to run at a Continuous Interval of two minutes, so that we can see scheduling in action. (But, of course, only do this if you are working on a test system which is either all installed on a single machine, or at the very least is on a test network. Please don't schedule Business View at two minute intervals on an operational system and/or network and then blame us!)

Testing a schedule

Close the Business View notebook and promote 'Penguin' to Production status.

Go to the Work in Progress window from Operations in the Warehouses notebook and keep a close eye on the entries.

You should see 'Penguin' scheduled to be run.

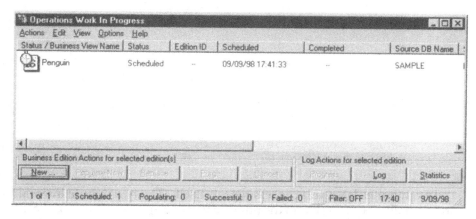

When the chosen time arrives, it will appear on the screen labeled as 'Populating'.

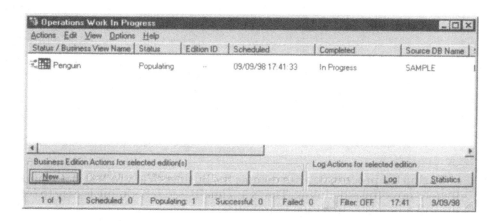

If you've already run this Business View, you'll see the earlier version labeled as 'Purging', and it will then disappear. The new version then displays the 'Successful' message, and the next scheduled run is also shown. (There's more about the various states a Business View can attain below.)

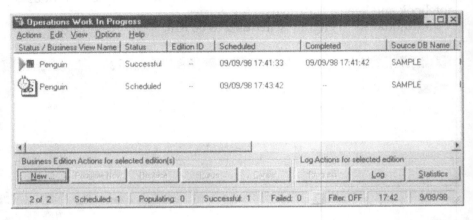

Two minutes later, this process repeats itself. (The two minute interval, incidentally, is counted from the time the view completes). This shot shows the purging of the first version of 'Penguin' and the populating of the second.

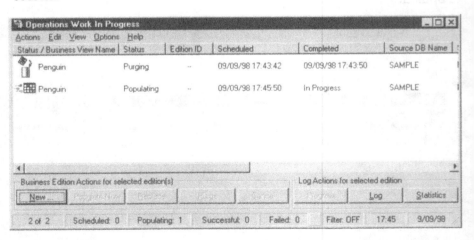

To stop the process, you can demote the Business View to Test status and then remove the scheduling. That's it; Time-Based scheduling is easy to set up and administer in Visual Warehouse.

Cascade scheduling

We touched briefly on the fact that one Business View can call another when we looked at the Scheduling page in the Business View notebook. Now we'll show you how to set this up.

First, some ground rules:

- Schedules can only be added or modified in Business Views that are in Development or Test status.

- However, Business Views have to have Production status before they will perform cascade scheduling.

The result is that we will have to swap between these two states during this exercise, but it isn't a problem because you'll have to do this when developing a real system so it's good practice.

So, make sure that 'Penguin', 'Foo' and 'Baa' are all in Test status and that all existing scheduling for them has been removed.

Starts on Success and Started by on Success

❻ *Note that, in Version 3.2 of Visual Warehouse, only two of the options described here are available: Starts and Started by. The four covered here, available from version 5.2, give a lot more flexibility to your schedules.* ❾

Go to the Schedule page in the Business View notebook for 'Penguin' and select the Starts on Success schedule type.

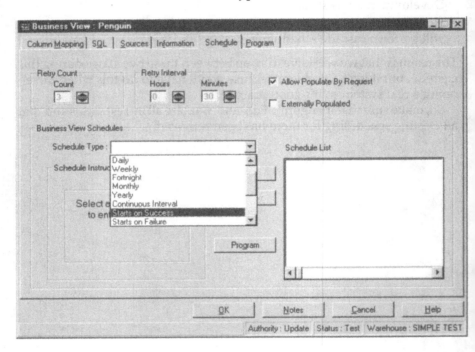

Highlight 'Foo' in the list of Business Views and click Add to place the schedule in the Schedule List.

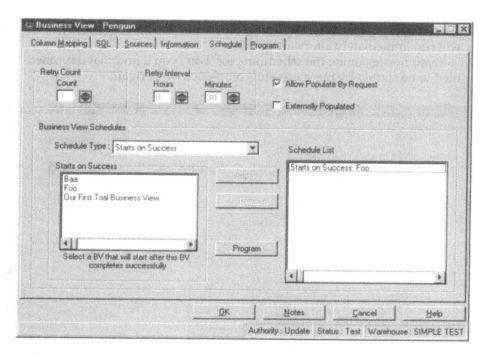

Click OK to finish. Now promote both 'Penguin' and 'Foo' to Production status and open the Work In Progress window. From there, click on the New button and run 'Penguin'.

'Penguin' should run first, purging any existing version and populating afresh; if this process is completed successfully, immediately thereafter 'Foo' should run in the same way.

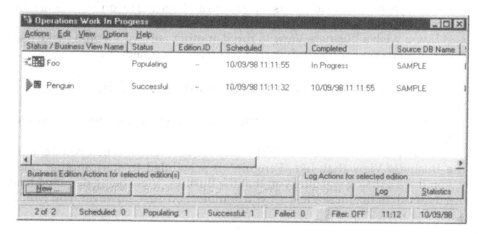

Clever, isn't it? Hereafter, whenever 'Penguin' is run successfully, 'Foo' will run immediately afterwards.

If you now examine the scheduling for 'Foo', you'll find that it is scheduled to be started by the successful completion of 'Penguin'

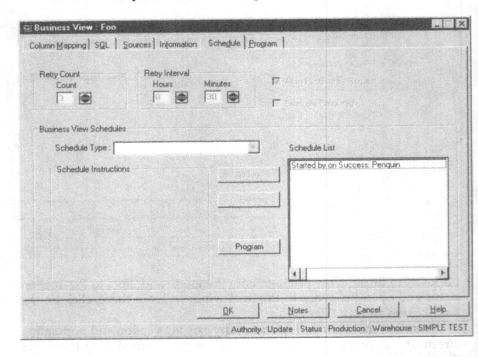

and in fact you could have defined the relationship between the two Business Views here instead. Starts on Success and Started by on Success are, in effect, different ends of the same process.

If you wish a Business View to run if another fails, you would make use of the Starts on Failure and Started by on Failure schedules.

Concurrently Starts and Concurrently Started By

Concurrently Starts and Concurrently Started By are also two ends of the same process.

Demote both 'Penguin' and 'Foo' back to Test status. When you demote a Business View that, like 'Penguin', is scheduled to start another one, you'll see a dialog warning you that the Business View being demoted has a dependent Business View. (If you demote 'Foo' first, however, you won't see the warning).

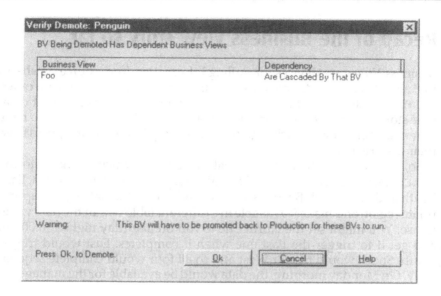

You can go ahead with the demotion, of course, by clicking OK; the dialog is just to ensure you're aware that, once this view loses Production status, dependent views will not be started automatically.

Once again, move to the Schedule tab for 'Foo', select Concurrently Starts and choose the Business View 'Baa'. This means, as you might expect, that as soon as 'Foo' is started (by whatever means) 'Baa' will also start at the same time.

Promote all three Business Views to Production status and start 'Penguin'. It should populate and then both 'Foo' and 'Baa' should start at almost the same time ('Foo' will lead, but only just).

You have probably got the idea by now – you can chain a series of Business Views together so that they act in concert, processing your data in whatever sequence you require.

Now might be a good time for a recap.

Recap of the Business View story so far

Business Views are devices for pulling information from source databases that already exist within your organization – for example, a database called SALES that stores all of the sales made by your organization. If that database stores every sale it may run to billions of individual records. You have four managers, one for each region, who are only interested in figures from their own regions.

So, you set up a Source in Visual Warehouse which connects to the SALES database. Then you would create four Business Views – North, East, South and West. Each Business View would extract the data for the appropriate region and make it available in a different table within the data warehouse. You might set the North one to run on Saturday night at 6:00 pm and get it to trigger the East one when it completes. East would trigger South, South would trigger West and so all four would complete sequentially. On Monday morning, the data would be available for the managers.

Chapter 6

More about Business Views

Business Views are clever

By the end of the last chapter you will have realized how powerful and flexible Business Views can be, but they get cleverer yet.

Business Views can act as sources for other Business Views

Suppose that your four Business Views not only extracted the relevant data, but also summarized it in some way (summarizing data is covered in Chapter 7). Suppose further that the CEO of the company also wants an overview of what is happening in the company. Rather than go back to the source database again, there is nothing to stop you building a Business View for the CEO that uses data from the tables you have just created in the data warehouse.

We can demonstrate this using 'Penguin', 'Foo' and 'Baa'. OK, so there are only three of them, but if we can do it with three, you will probably believe that it would be possible with four.

First, demote 'Baa' to Test status.

Then, from the Business View window for SIMPLE TEST

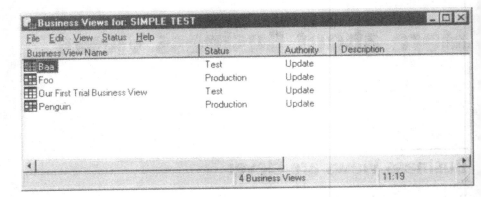

select File, New to create a new Business View. Call it 'CEO' and select SIMPLE TEST as the Source. The available tables that appear include 'Penguin', 'Foo' and 'Baa',

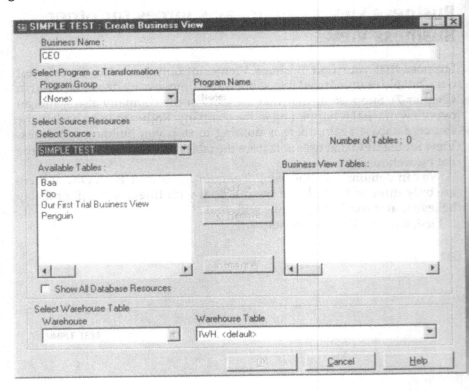

so add all three to the list of Business View tables.

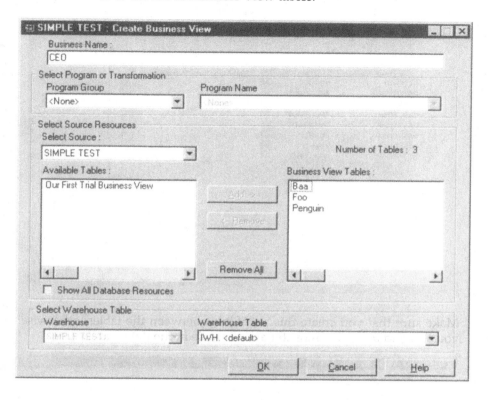

Click on OK and you can create the detail of the Business View. Choose the set of columns as shown below.

1	DEPTNO	'Baa'
2	PROJNAME	'Baa'
3	EMPNO	'Foo'
4	FIRSTNME	'Foo'
5	LASTNAME	'Foo'
6	WORKDEPT	'Foo'
7	DEPTNO1 *(You're prompted to re-name this one to distinguish it from the* DEPTNO *field from 'Baa')*	'Penguin'
8	DEPTNAME	'Penguin'

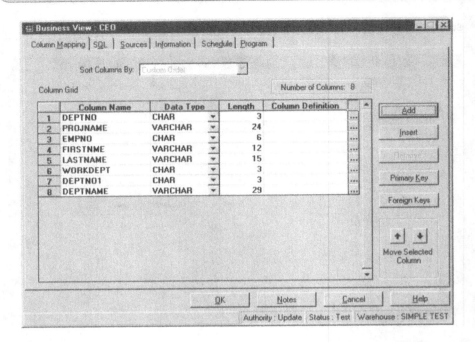

Make sure that you create this set of joins between the tables, otherwise you will end up with a monster answer table in the data warehouse.

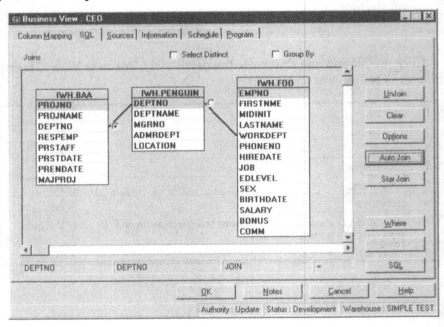

Then move to the schedule tab. Here you can set 'CEO' to be Started by on Success of 'Baa' (which means that it runs after 'Baa' has completed successfully),

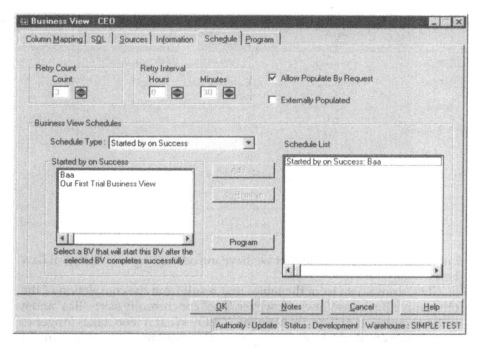

just to demonstrate that this Business View is no different from the others and can be scheduled in the same way. Finally, click on OK.

Promote 'Baa' and 'CEO' to Production status, and try manually running 'Penguin' again; this should cascade 'Foo', then 'Baa' and finally 'CEO'. With any luck this should work,

Status / Business View Name	Status	Edition ID	Scheduled	Completed	Source DB Name
Baa	Successful	--	10/09/98 11:29:52	10/09/98 11:30:26	SAMPLE
CEO	Populating	--	10/09/98 11:30:26	In Progress	VWTARG
Foo	Successful	--	10/09/98 11:29:51	10/09/98 11:30:25	SAMPLE
Penguin	Successful	--	10/09/98 11:29:25	10/09/98 11:29:51	SAMPLE

but it is interesting to note that we have introduced a possible logical flaw here.

'CEO' draws data from the tables that result from the completion of the other three Business Views. However, 'Foo' concurrently starts 'Baa' and it is the completion of 'Baa' that triggers 'CEO'. What if 'Foo' takes longer to complete than 'Baa'? As we have set up the sequence here, 'CEO' might one day try to pull data from a table that was in the process of being rebuilt. In a production system it would be better to have 'Foo' simply start 'Baa' rather than start it concurrently.

We only make this point because it is possible to build a system that works in test (as does this one) but then fails later as the table sizes change.

This ability to chain Business Views together, and the ability to treat a Business View as a source of data for another Business View is incredibly powerful. The only problem, you might think, is trying to keep an overview of how they all interact. That is clearly what the good people at IBM thought you might think, which is why they provided Tree Views.

Tree Views

If you open the Business View window for SIMPLE TEST and open the
View menu, you will find two options for Tree view.

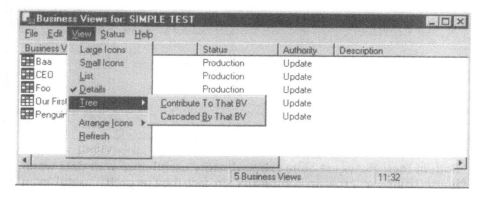

The first one will show which Business Views contribute to the current one.
As you can see, this highlights the fact that three different Business Views
contribute to 'CEO'.

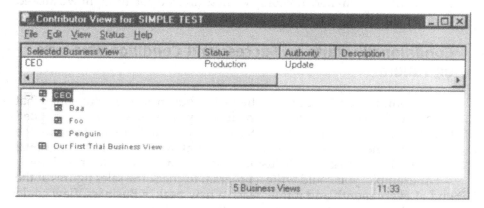

The other view shows you the Cascade chain that we have set up.

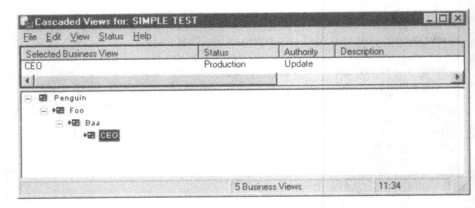

Both of these views are quite extraordinarily useful once your data warehouse begins to grow in complexity (in fact they're pretty useful even when it is small).

So, we have finished looking at scheduling. The astute reader will have noticed that we have avoided the last options for scheduling, namely Conditionally Starts on Success and Conditionally Starts on Failure, so we'll mention them here for completeness (in case you thought we missed them by mistake).

Conditionally Starts on Success and Conditionally Starts on Failure

These sound like yet others in the series, but in fact they're somewhat different. If you select these schedule types, a dialog opens entitled Cascade Program. Here you can attach a program to be processed once the current Business View has completed. This allows you to add conditional control to the processing of a Business View, or of multiple Business Views.

For example, you could write a program to check the sales figures at the end of every month and if they reach a new peak, a Business View could run to identify any star performers in the sales teams.

We're not going to do this as an example, because we are only trying to give you an overview of the main features. However, bear in mind that this feature is available if and when you need it.

❝ Version 3.1 had just one conditional schedule type, called Conditionally Starts. ❞

Editions

Edition: a whole new word in the Visual Warehouse repertoire. Business Views have editions, and an edition is a point-in-time view of the data generated by that Business View. Editions are particularly helpful when you want to build up a picture of trends over a period of time.

For instance, suppose you have a Business View to extract data that is scheduled to run on the last day of each month. If you specify that there should be twelve editions of this Business View, at the end of the year you will have twelve snapshots of that data, and these can be used to determine trends. At the end of the thirteenth month, the first edition is deleted and re-created with current data, so you always have a full year's data on hand.

Setting the number of editions

Create a new Business View called 'Ed' which simply pulls the entire DEPARTMENT table into the data warehouse.

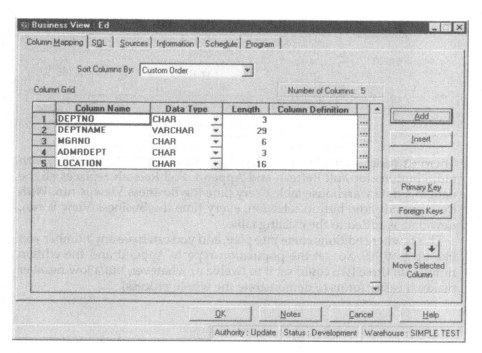

'Ed' appears with Development status, which is perfect for our current needs because it so happens that you can only make changes to the number of editions in a Business View that has Development (as opposed to Test or Production) status.

Double click 'Ed' to get the Business View notebook and select the Information tab.

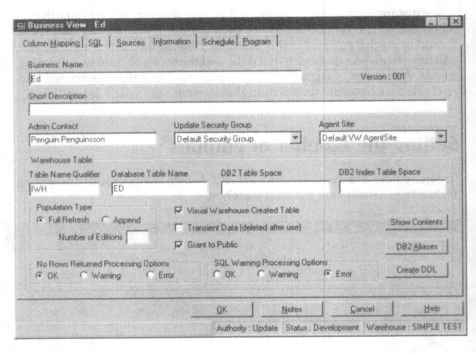

There's a panel on the lower left hand side labeled Population Type, with radio buttons for Full Refresh and Append. Full Refresh replaces all the data in a data warehouse table every time the Business View is run. With the Append radio button selection, every time the Business View is run, new data is added to the existing table.

This is where editions come into play, and you can have any number you like up to 9,999. So, set the population type to Append and the edition number to three (we could set it to twelve or whatever, but a low number makes it easier for us to demonstrate the whole process).

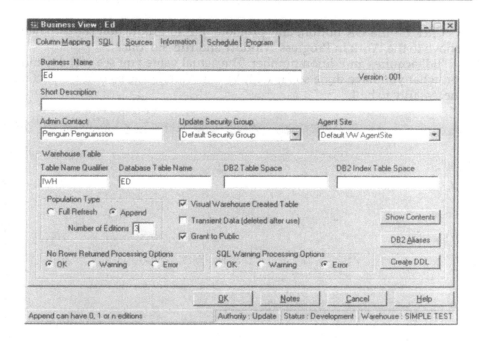

If you now move back to the Column Mapping Tab you'll find that a new column has been added.

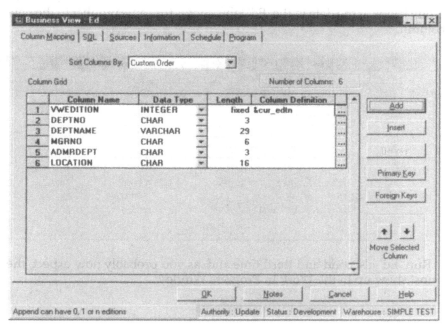

Click on the OK button, and promote 'Ed' to Production status. Then move to the Work In Progress Window and run 'Ed' once.

'Ed' acquires an Edition number. The actual value you see will depend on what you have done so far with Visual Warehouse, so don't expect it necessarily to be 1.

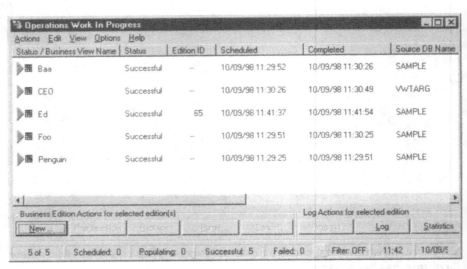

A quick look at the data in the 'Ed' table shows the same number in the new column.

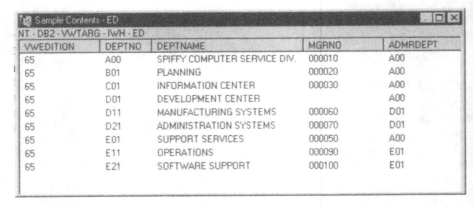

Run 'Ed' a second and third time and, as you probably now expect, the 'runs' show up in the Work In Progress Window

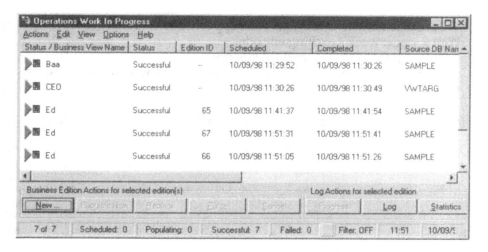

and the process simply adds data to the table in the data warehouse.

VWEDITION	DEPTNO	DEPTNAME	MGRNO	ADMRDEPT
65	A00	SPIFFY COMPU...	000010	A00
65	B01	PLANNING	000020	A00
65	C01	INFORMATION ...	000030	A00
65	D01	DEVELOPMEN...		A00
65	D11	MANUFACTURI...	000060	D01
65	D21	ADMINISTRATI...	000070	D01
65	E01	SUPPORT SER...	000050	A00
65	E11	OPERATIONS	000090	E01
65	E21	SOFTWARE SU...	000100	E01
66	A00	SPIFFY COMPU...	000010	A00
66	B01	PLANNING	000020	A00
66	C01	INFORMATION ...	000030	A00
66	D01	DEVELOPMEN...		A00
66	D11	MANUFACTURI...	000060	D01
66	D21	ADMINISTRATI...	000070	D01
66	E01	SUPPORT SER...	000050	A00
66	E11	OPERATIONS	000090	E01
66	E21	SOFTWARE SU...	000100	E01
67	A00	SPIFFY COMPU...	000010	A00
67	B01	PLANNING	000020	A00
67	C01	INFORMATION	000030	A00
67	D01	DEVELOPMEN...		A00
67	D11	MANUFACTURI...	000060	D01
67	D21	ADMINISTRATI...	000070	D01
67	E01	SUPPORT SER...	000050	A00
67	E11	OPERATIONS	000090	E01
67	E21	SOFTWARE SU...	000100	E01

But excitement mounts! What will happen when we run it a fourth time? Wait for next week's exciting episode!

Too long to wait? OK, we'll tell you now.

After the fourth run, the Work In Progress Window shows only the last three 'runs'

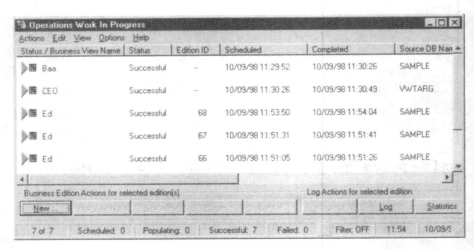

and the data in the table only holds the data from the last three runs.

VWEDITION	DEPTNO	DEPTNAME	MGRNO	ADMRDEPT
68	A00	SPIFFY COMPU...	000010	A00
68	B01	PLANNING	000020	A00
68	C01	INFORMATION ...	000030	A00
68	D01	DEVELOPMEN...		A00
68	D11	MANUFACTURI...	000060	D01
68	D21	ADMINISTRATI...	000070	D01
68	E01	SUPPORT SER...	000050	A00
68	E11	OPERATIONS ...	000090	E01
68	E21	SOFTWARE SU...	000100	E01
66	A00	SPIFFY COMPU...	000010	A00
66	B01	PLANNING	000020	A00
66	C01	INFORMATION ...	000030	A00
66	D01	DEVELOPMEN...		A00
66	D11	MANUFACTURI...	000060	D01
66	D21	ADMINISTRATI...	000070	D01
66	E01	SUPPORT SER...	000050	A00
66	E11	OPERATIONS ...	000090	E01
66	E21	SOFTWARE SU...	000100	E01
67	A00	SPIFFY COMPU...	000010	A00
67	B01	PLANNING	000020	A00
67	C01	INFORMATION ...	000030	A00
67	D01	DEVELOPMEN...		A00
67	D11	MANUFACTURI...	000060	D01
67	D21	ADMINISTRATI...	000070	D01
67	E01	SUPPORT SER...	000050	A00
67	E11	OPERATIONS ...	000090	E01
67	E21	SOFTWARE SU...	000100	E01

Sample Contents - ED
NT - DB2 - VWTARG - IWH - ED

Close

❝ *As an aside, the numbers shown in the* VWEDITION *column are important only in that their values show the sequence in which the editions were created. In fact, had we run other Business Views in the interim, the numbers wouldn't even be consecutive. What is important is that these numbers allow you to identify the edition from which the records in the table are derived.* ❞

We chose this particular example because it demonstrates clearly how editions work, but we would never suggest that it represents a particularly sensible use of editions. As with so much that Visual Warehouse offers, this is an excellent feature that's highly versatile. How you use it is up to you, but certain possibilities spring immediately to mind.

You might schedule a Business View to run once a month. That Business View could summarize some aspect of your business into a single record, and one column in that table could contain the name of the month, and another the year. The VWEDITION column could be made invisible to the users who would simply see, every time they used the table, the last twelve month's business summary.

The foregoing illustrates further the power of Business Views (and Editions), but there's more yet, as you'll see in the next chapter.

Chapter 7

Business Views for data transformation

Data transformation

'Data transformation' is a broad term that embraces all of the changes that you can make to the data as it is imported into the warehouse. Some of these changes have already been covered – for example, by selecting certain fields from a table and rejecting others you have already performed a level of data transformation.

As a DBA and DWA, there are others that you're just itching to make. You want to be able to select from a table only those sales records where the Region field has the value 'North'.

Given that data warehouses frequently store summaries of data rather than all of the raw data, you just know that you are going to want to group the records by certain similar characteristics in some fields, whilst summing or counting the values in others. For example, suppose you have five years' worth of sales data that equates to millions/billions of records. You are unlikely to want that level of detail in the data warehouse because none of the data warehouse users will want to find a particular sales record. Instead those users may want to see the total sales, per month, for different classes of goods in different regions.

You can probably see where we are going here – we have been (unsubtly) dropping SQL key words into these descriptions – Select, Where, Group...By, Sum, Count. It will hopefully come as no surprise that all of the data transformation performed by Visual Warehouse is done by means of SQL.

We have no intention of trying to teach you SQL here. For a start you are probably familiar with the language. If not then we are delighted to point you at the book entitled 'Inside Relational Databases' mentioned in the introduction, a large chunk of which is devoted to SQL.

What we will do is show you where within Visual Warehouse you can use SQL skills to transform the incoming data.

Creating a Business View to transform data

From the list of Business Views for SIMPLE TEST, highlight 'CEO', pop down the Edit menu and select copy. A dialog appears which you can modify to produce a copy of 'CEO' called 'CEO2'.

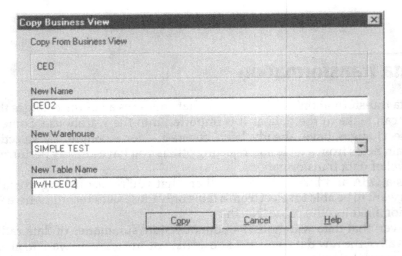

As in most forms of software development, copying existing work like this is useful for speeding up development (and also for protecting current achievements from being accidentally destroyed).

'CEO2' will appear with Development status, so promote it to Test status. Then double click it and move to the SQL tab.

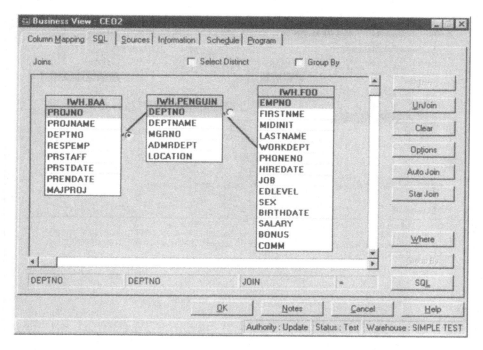

❧ *For reasons discussed in Chapter 3, we are using Visual Warehouse version 3.1 for screen shots of these windows.* ❧

Click on the SQL button and, after a brief visit from a dialog asking you to save the view, some SQL appears.

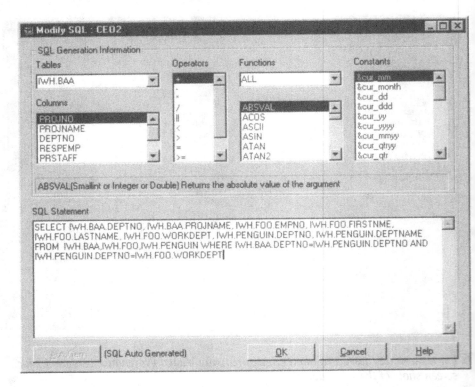

Notice that, by studying the bottom left hand corner, you can tell that this SQL code is auto-generated. This means that Visual Warehouse is using the selections you have made so far, and from them generating this code which in turn will be used to perform the import of data into the data warehouse. If you flip back to the SQL tab, you can try playing around with the interface. For example, each join has a radio button. If you select the 'Penguin-Foo' join

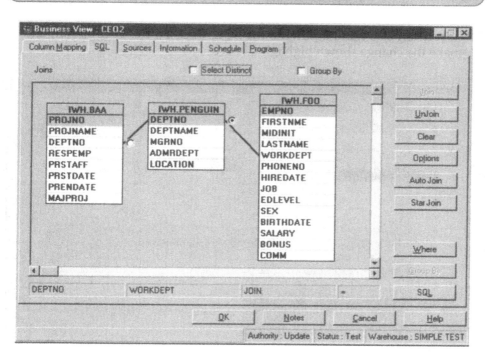

the details of this join appear towards the bottom of the window. By pressing the Options button, you can alter the properties of this join.

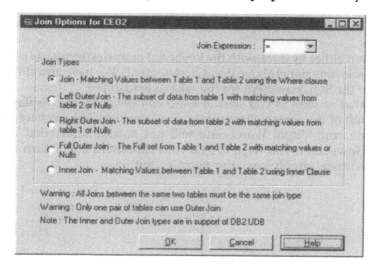

Again, from the SQL tab you can use the Where button to add a Where clause and a Group By button to add...well, surely you can guess!

You can also hand edit/write the SQL. Click on the SLQ button, and make the change shown highlighted here

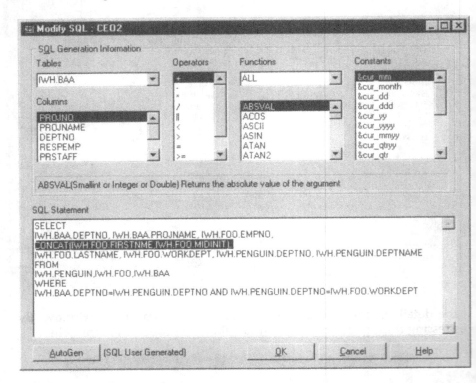

(which can either by done with the keyboard or by dexterous use of mouse and the selection panel above the SQL statement). We have also altered the layout of the SQL statement for the sake of readability.

Note that as soon as you start to hand edit the code, the display at the bottom left of the screen alters subtly. You have now taken charge of the SQL code, and Visual Warehouse will not auto-generate that code in future. However, if you want to lose your alterations and return to auto-generated code, simply push the AutoGen button.

The change we have made simply concatenates the first name and middle initial, as you can see if you populate the data warehouse using the Business View.

DEPTNO	PROJNAME	EMPNO	FIRSTNME	LASTNAME
E01	WELD LINE PL	000020	MICHAEL L	THOMPSON
C01	QUERY SERVI	000030	SALLYXXXXA	KWAN
C01	QUERY SERVI	000140	HEATHER A	NICHOLLS
C01	QUERY SERVI	000130	DOLORES M	QUINTANA
C01	USER EDUCAT	000030	SALLYXXXXA	KWAN
C01	USER EDUCAT	000140	HEATHER A	NICHOLLS
C01	USER EDUCAT	000130	DOLORES M	QUINTANA
D11	W L PROGRAM	000060	IRVING F	STERN
D11	W L PROGRAM	000220	JENNIFER K	LUTZ
D11	W L PROGRAM	000210	WILLIAM T	JONES
D11	W L PROGRAM	000200	DAVID	BROWN
D11	W L PROGRAM	000190	JAMES H	WALKER
D11	W L PROGRAM	000180	MARILYN S	SCOUTTEN
D11	W L PROGRAM	000170	MASATOSHIJ	YOSHIMURA
D11	W L PROGRAM	000160	ELIZABETHR	PIANKA
D11	W L PROGRAM	000150	BRUCE	ADAMSON
D11	W L PROD CO	000060	IRVING F	STERN
D11	W L PROD CO	000220	JENNIFER K	LUTZ

Record: 1 of 90

This highlights an oddity of the data in SAMPLE, namely that the First Names in the EMPLOYEE table have variable numbers of trailing spaces. On the other hand, perhaps oddity is the wrong word. The sad truth is that data in operational databases is frequently inconsistent, which in turn is why we often need to either fix the data in the source database, or devise some form of data transformation that will provide the required consistency.

We'll have a look at one more type of data transformation, this time using the Column Mapping tab. Create a new Business View that uses DB2 SAMPLE DATA as the Source and PROJECT as the Business View table; this is how the Source tab should look.

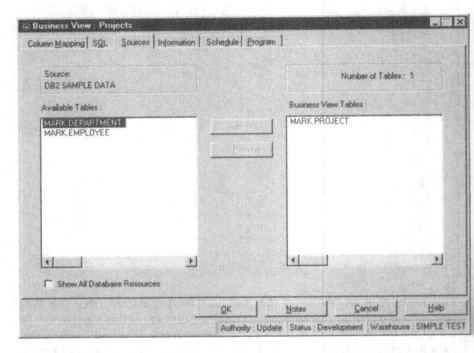

The PROJECT table happens to have two date fields – PRENDATE and PRSTDATE (presumably Project end and start dates respectively). We are going to get the Business View to create a table in the data warehouse that lists the projects, together with their length in days.

From the Column Mapping tab use the Add button to add the DEPTNO column, then use the Insert button to add a column called LENGTH. When this is done, click on the ellipsis button to the right of the Column Definition column and the following dialog appears.

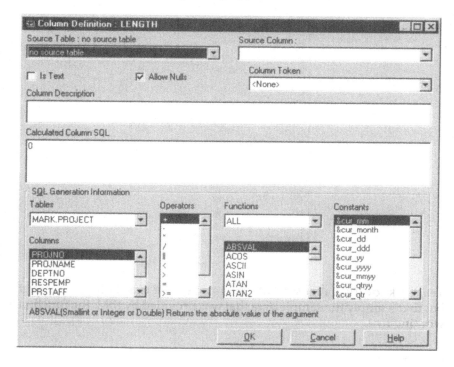

Enter the following:

```
DAYS (MARK.PROJECT.PRENDATE) -
    DAYS (MARK.PROJECT.PRSTDATE)
```

as the Calculated Column SQL. This uses the DAYS function to calculate the DAY value for each date and then the difference between the two.

Running the Business View produces a table like this.

DEPTNO	LENGTH
D01	396
D21	396
D21	396
D21	396
D21	396
C01	396
C01	396
D01	396
D11	396
D11	334
D11	334
D11	289
E01	396
E11	396
E01	396
E21	396
E21	396
E21	396
E21	396

Sample Contents - PROJECTS
NT - DB2 - VWTARG - IWH - PROJECTS

Yes, we know that almost all of the projects have exactly the same length, but that's simply the sample data that was provided by IBM; the function is working fine.

Transformers

Visual Warehouse 5.2 comes with a collection of ready-defined data transformations, including those for various statistical processes. The Calculate Statistics transformer, for instance, can sum, calculate average, variance, standard deviation and so on, and there are also transformers for reformatting date fields and for calculating subtotals.

Transformers are accessed from the Program tab of a Business View. Certain selections have to be made before a transformer will run, and these differ between transformers. The help system lists these

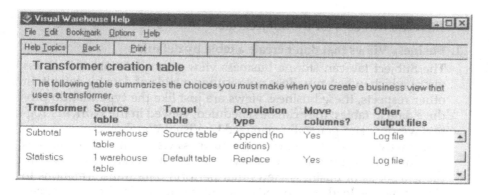

and also described each transformer in detail.

Transformers are written in Java, and you'll need to install the Java Developer's Kit (JDK) that comes on the Visual Warehouse CD-ROM before you can make use of them.

Summary

Transforming data is a further string to the bow of a Business View, and an extremely important string it is too. A data warehouse is like any database: you only put data in so that you can get information out. Data transformations are the way to ensure that only good stuff goes in so that only good stuff comes out.

Data can only divulge useful information if that data is in a usable format. Data transformation, implemented through the medium of Business Views, ensures that only clean and orderly data makes its way into your warehouse, and that sensible responses will be given when you ask questions of it.

The two areas briefly covered below, Subjects and Visual Warehouse Programs, are both useful when you're working on more complex data transformations.

Subjects

The third tab in the Warehouse desktop is labeled Subjects. (OK, so it's the first tab on the left, but we've already met the Warehouses and Sources tabs.) It's an important area but one over which we shall be skimming lightly because it will be of most use to you once your warehouse has grown and flourished.

There are two uses for the Subjects tab:

1. **Business Views that don't create a table by default**

   The Subject tab can store a business view or a collection of business views which, when run, does not result in a table of data by default. In other respects, these business views are just like the type that do produce data in tables: they can be scheduled, viewed in the Work in Progress window and generally managed by Visual Warehouse.

   But why would you want such a business view? The main reason is that sometimes you don't actually want a table of data created. An example is a series of business views that perform data transformations to clean data, and load and unload data into existing tables. You don't need interim tables, you just need the cleaned data to be popped into its proper place.

2. **Collections of Business Views from multiple warehouses**

   Business views from different warehouses can be stored together in the Subject tab. It's useful to do this if you have business views that cover the same sort of ground in separate warehouses, ones that work with financial data, for instance. Keeping them together as a Subject means they're all in one place and easily accessible should you need to perform any updating or maintenance tasks.

Visual Warehouse programs

Sometimes you need more power and flexibility in your Business Views than that which it's possible to build within Visual Warehouse.

❝ *As a beginner in the field, the preceding sentence may have already switched you off. That's quite fair; you won't need this when you're just starting.* ❞

Business Views can make use of programs in two ways:

- by running a program instead of the SQL code associated with the Business View, or
- by running the program after the Business View has completed.

Programs can be written in any language that produces executable files, batch files or DLLs, and can perform tasks such as data cleansing operations or other forms of data manipulations. A program that runs after a Business View has completed can be a powerful tool; when the Business View completes successfully the program can interrogate the populated table and, based on the results, run a further Business View.

This sort of program is termed a conditional cascade schedule program: this might sound familiar if you've encountered the Conditionally Starts schedule type and the Cascade Program dialog in Chapter 6.

A collection of ready-made programs is supplied with Visual Warehouse (select the Sample Visual Warehouse programs book from the list of topics in the help system) for various common data loading and exporting tasks.

More summary

Business Views are all about power and flexibility and they form the heart of Visual Warehouse's functionality. Our examples have of necessity been simple, but combined with the accompanying text they should give you an idea of what can be achieved.

Chapter 8

The Work in Progress Window

The Work in Progress Window

This window, as you've already seen, displays details about the processing of Business Views. Not only can you see things that are currently happening, but from here you can also inspect the log files that record all actions in Visual Warehouse for a particular Business View (or indeed, for a particular 'Edition' of a Business View. Editions are covered in Chapter 6).

You can reach the Work In Progress window from the Visual Warehouse desktop by popping down the Operations menu and selecting Work In Progress.

As a DWA, you would expect to spend a lot of time with this window, visiting every half day at the very least. WIP is what lets you put your finger on the pulse of the system so that you can keep things ticking along nicely. The WIP view also gives you the chance to spot failed Business Views before users do, so you are aware of the problem, or even have solved it, before they contact you – a welcome boost for the self-esteem.

Status

The first column is labeled Status/Business View Name. The latter part is self-explanatory, and the status is shown by various icons. It's not instantly apparent that these icons are, in fact, translated into text form in the second column, headed "Status".

Nonetheless, the various status ratings might benefit from a little amplification.

Successful

This is the one we all want to see. It signifies that everything went as it should.

Each green triangle to the left of a Successful icon represents a table or an entry in the warehouse. If you purge (delete) one from the WIP window, the associated data will be deleted from the warehouse. Either the whole table will go or, in the case of an edition of a Business View, the data from that edition will be deleted from the table.

Scheduled

This says that the Business View edition is scheduled and waiting to be processed.

Failed

Trouble. The Business View edition has failed for some reason during processing.

Warning

This tells you that one or more warning messages were generated during the processing. These can be SQL messages and/or messages reporting that the data was not located in the source table.

Canceling & Canceled

When the first of these icons appears, a user has canceled the processing of the Business View edition. The second is visible while a Business View edition is being canceled.

Populating

This one appears while a Business View edition is actually populating the target table with data.

Purging

Shows that processed data is being purged (expunged) from the target table.

Retrying

If there is a communication failure while a Business View edition is processing, it will be tried again (depending on the settings). This icon is visible during retrying.

Scheduled, Completed

These two columns show the time a Business View edition was scheduled to start and the time at which it finished.

Source DB Name, etc.

The next six columns identify the source and target databases and types, the resource name and the Agent Site.

Retry

The final column, Retry, shows the number of times the process has been retried.

Work in Progress

The Work in Progress window, apart from displaying scheduling information, is a mine of further details about how and when Business Views run. Statistics are a useful aid to troubleshooting and can tell you if a Business View took an unreasonable time to run, or whether it transferred an unlikely amount of data. A whistle-stop tour is therefore in order.

Statistics

To see this information, open the Work in Progress window and click the Statistics button in the bottom right hand corner.

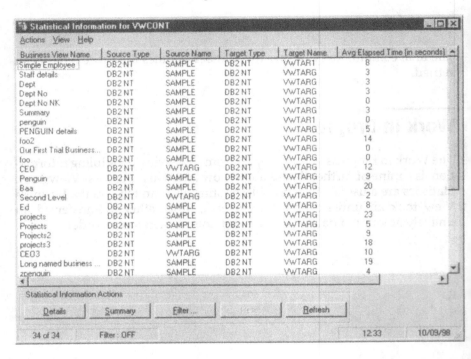

In the Statistical Information window is a list of all the Business Views with the type and name for both source and target, average running speed and size in bytes. To see even more detail, highlight a view in the list and click the Details button and a further window is displayed.

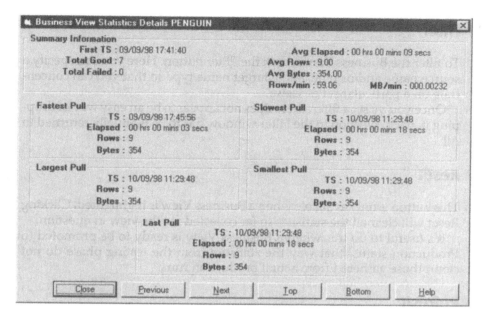

(If a Business View was highlighted in the Work in Progress window when you clicked the Statistics button, this window would have opened automatically, immediately after the Statistical Information window opened.)

The information is set out clearly on the screen, giving a summary of the Business View editions. Below this is a closer inspection of the fastest and slowest times in which the Business View ran, details of the largest and smallest amounts of data it moved, and finally, the last time an edition of the Business View was processed. If a Business View has only run once, the Fastest Pull, Slowest Pull, Largest Pull and Smallest Pull are not shown.

The "TS" (Time Stamp) that's quoted in all these details is the date and time that the edition finished processing.

You can navigate through the views listed in the Statistical Information window with the Previous, Next, Top and Bottom buttons.

Click Close to return the aforementioned window.

Summary

The Summary button shows similar information but for the Business Views taken as a whole.

Filter

To filter the Business Views, click the Filter button. Here you can specify a source name and/or type, and a target name/type so that you can concentrate on a particular set of views.

Once you've set a filter, there does not appear to be an easy way of dropping it. Each selection in the Filter window has to be manually returned to All.

Reset

This button is only available when a Business View is highlighted. Clicking Reset will clear all the statistics so far collected for the view in question.

It's useful to do this when a Business View is ready to be promoted to Production status: that way the statistics from the testing phase do not cloud those gathered from actual production runs.

Refresh

Updates the statistical displays.

Log

Close the Statistical Information window to return to the WIP window. At the bottom, alongside the Statistics button, is a button labeled Log. Click it to make the acquaintance of an area that's very important to DWAs everywhere. As you'll see, clicking the Log button shows you a list of the Business Views.

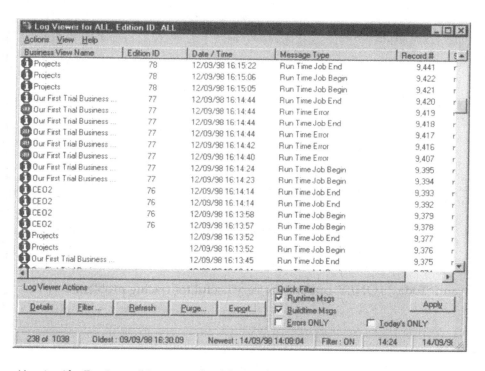

(Again, if a Business View was highlighted in the WIP window when you clicked the Log button, you'd see the log for that particular Business View).

137

The check boxes settings default to showing runtime and buildtime messages, but the 'Errors ONLY'

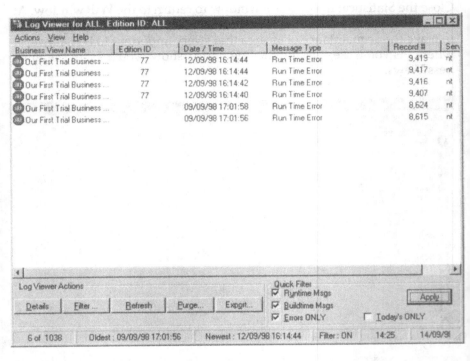

and 'Today's ONLY' options are very useful for tracing problems.

Clicking the Log button with a particular Business View highlighted gives a more detailed log for the actions of that view.

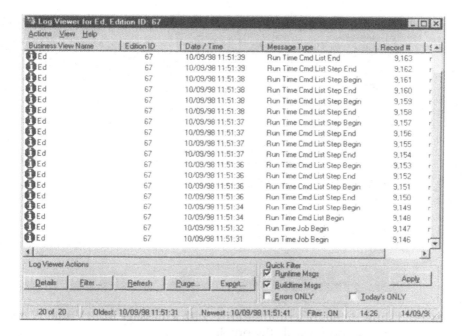

If a Business View should fail, the first place you should look to find out what's gone wrong is at the log.

If you highlighted a failed Business View (one with a red octagonal Stop sign) and clicked the Details button...

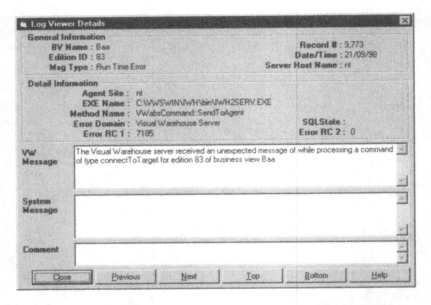

it would show details of a runtime error with a message from Visual Warehouse pointing you towards the problem.

The Log window gives access to a great deal of information about what's happened, and this is invaluable for trouble shooting and problem solving.

Progress

Also accessible from the WIP window is the Progress button. This button
displays details of each step in the processing of a business view; the button
becomes available as soon as a view is selected in the Work in Progress
window. It can be used either after a business view has completed, or while
the view is actually proceeding, as it was for the screen shot shown below.

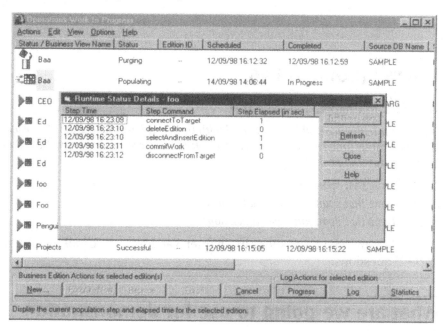

❧ *You can also get to this information by simply double clicking the Business View in
the WIP window.* ❧

Summary

You have just been introduced to two very important areas, the Work in
Progress window and the Log files. Both give you tools for ensuring the
smooth running of the system, by reporting the status of Business Views,
and, when something goes wrong, giving very full details of what problem
(or problems) were encountered. It is well worth while spending time
becoming familiar with both these areas, as you're likely to visit them
frequently once you have a live system.

Chapter 9

Data from disparate sources

Solving problem two

Way back in Chapter 1 we said that:

Business Intelligence enables you to deal with three fundamental classes of problem and that those problems could be characterized as three types of question that managers typically asked:

1. *Questions that span time*
2. *Questions that span disparate data sources*
3. *Questions that span multiple dimensions*

We dealt with 'type 1' questions in Chapter 3 and here we'll look at solving 'type 2' questions.

What are we going to use for demonstration purposes?

We have shown you how to pull data from a DB2 source. We could combine that with data from another DB2 database, but that would be unimaginative. We could combine it with data from another common database (say, Oracle) but that would only be helpful for those readers who have Oracle. So, we'll use another format that is both versatile and easy to distribute – a text file. Almost every data storage application can output and import data in text format and the value of a flat file as a common denominator is exploited by Visual Warehouse. It enables you to reach data regardless of whether it's stored in LIMS on Linux, dBASE on DOS or Pastrami on Rye (hold the pickles).

What do you need to know before we get ' started?

As we hinted in Chapter 3, you don't really need to learn any new skills this wonder to perform, you just need one fundamental piece of information and you need to get your brain around a tiny bit of recursion. Oh, and you may need a bit of a recap, so we'll provide that first.

Recap

You already know how to pull data from a data source (for example, a company database) into the data warehouse. You use a Source and a Business View. The Source is used to identify the relevant tables (and possibly fields) in the data source. The Business View is essentially an SQL statement that joins the tables, queries them and writes the result to a table in the data warehouse.

The summary for Chapter 3 makes the point that a Source pulls data from only one source of data. Any given Business View can only pull data from one Source and write it to a table in the data warehouse. This appears to make it logically impossible to pull data from two different sources of data into one table in the data warehouse.

Fundamental information and recursion

However, we said in Chapter 3 that 'a Source points to a source of data (often a database)'. A source usually points to a database, but it can point to something else. It can, for example, point to a text file on a disk. It can also, crucially, point to a warehouse (which is where the recursion comes in). Now, remembering that a warehouse is a collection of Business Views, it follows that this gives us a way of pulling data together from disparate sources.

A quick example

Say, for example, that you create a warehouse called SIMPLE TEST (which, it so happens, you have). Within this warehouse you create a Business View called 'Foo' which contains the name, ID, department code etc. for your employees (you've done this as well).

EMPNO ·	FIRSTNME	MIDINIT	LASTNAME	WORKDEPT
000010	CHRISTINE	I	HAAS	A00
000020	MICHAEL	L	THOMPSON	B01
000030	SALLY	A	KWAN	C01
000050	JOHN	B	GEYER	E01
000060	IRVING	F	STERN	D11
000070	EVA	D	PULASKI	D21
000090	EILEEN	W	HENDERSON	E11
000100	THEODORE	Q	SPENSER	E21
000110	VINCENZO	G	LUCCHESSI	A00
and so on down to				
000340	JASON	R	GOUNOT	E21

(There are more columns in the table, we've deleted them from this view to save space.)

Now, suppose that you have a text file called, say, SALES.TXT that has been dumped from another DBMS of some kind and looks like this:

```
SALENO,ID,SALES
1,000110,34554
2,000110,34225
3,000110,35656
4,000050,59898
5,000060,45356
6,000070,3657
7,000110,567
...
30,000320,648
```

This shows the sales (measured in number of items per sale) made by given employees – Vincenzo Lucchessi (ID = 000110) seems to be a good salesman.

You want to be able to co-ordinate information from these two sources of data so that you can see who is actually making these sales. You might also want to perform a GROUP BY in order to see which department is selling the most.

You set up a Source and Business View within SIMPLE TEST that point to this file and bring it into the data warehouse. You now have two Business Views within SIMPLE TEST that point to data from different sources. If you create another Business View within SIMPLE TEST and tell it to use SIMPLE TEST as its Source, you will find that it can pull data from both of the Business Views that you have already created.

You should already have a Business View called 'Foo' that is fully functional. All we have to do is to create another Business View that points to the text file.

The practical bit

The text file called SALES.TXT is on the CD-ROM (see Appendix 3). You may want to move it to somewhere handier. For the sake of argument, we'll move it to the root directory C:\. (*If you want to play around with the contents of the file, don't forget it will be read-only when it is moved from the CD-ROM.*)

Creating a source for the text file

From the Sources desktop, choose File, New, Flat File LAN and click OK.

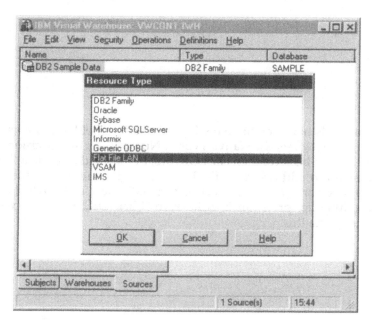

The window that opens has a General tab. Enter the Name as SALEINFO. In the Connection tab, select Local File. Then, in the Files tab, click New.

The File:New window also starts with a General tab. Fill in the full path and name of the flat file – C:\SALES.TXT. In the Parameters tab, set the File type to be comma, and click to add a check mark saying that the first row contains the column names.

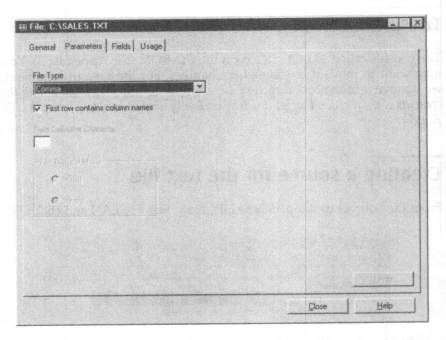

In the Fields tab, click the New button to add a field, and make Name equal to SalesNo, set the Native Type to Numeric, set the precision to be 5 and the scale to be zero; then click OK. Still in the Fields tab, click the New button again to add a second field. Set Name to EMPID and the Native Type to Varchar, Length 6. Click OK. Finally add a third Field called SALES, Numeric, precision 5, scale zero. Click OK, and your window should look like this.

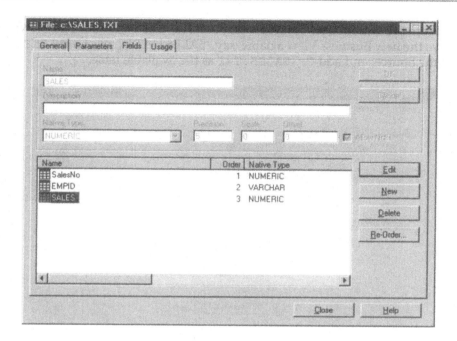

Close this window to return to the Flat File LAN window, and close this to return to the desktop.

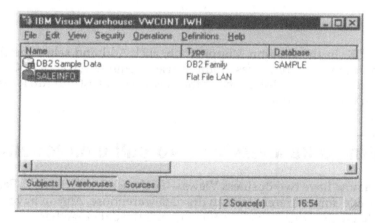

From the Warehouses desktop, open SIMPLE TEST and click File, New. Give the new Business View a name, say, 'SALES DATA', select SALEINFO as the Source, and add C:\SALES.TXT as the available table.

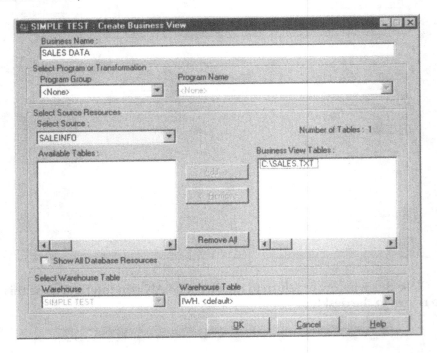

Click OK. In the Column Mapping tab, click Add and select the three columns. For testing purposes, nothing else is required, so click OK.

In the Business View list, promote the new view to Test and run it manually from the WIP window.

Creating a Business View to pull data together

OK, you now have two Business Views – 'Foo' and 'SALES DATA'. Each is 'responsible' for a different table in the data warehouse. All you have to do now is to create a third Business View to pull the data together.

It seems foolish to spell this step out in detail; it is simply another Business View. The only difference is that you need to choose SIMPLE TEST as the Source and make sure you add both tables. *OK, we admit it. The name for this Business View ('TooFoo') is facetious, but hey, who said Business Intelligence had to be serious?*

Choose the fields as shown

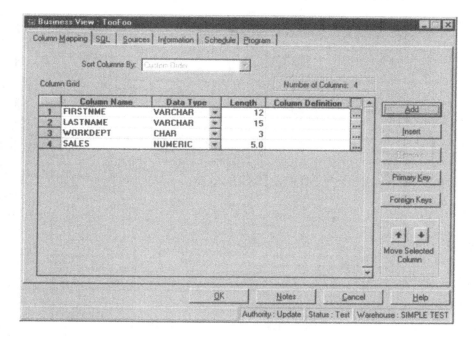

And set up the required join

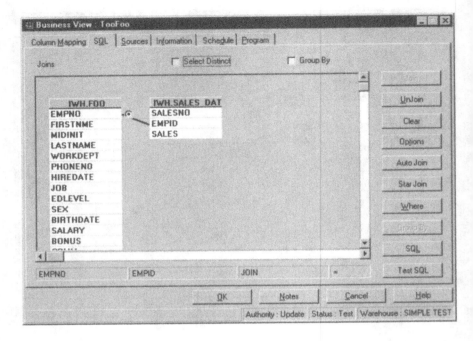

Save the Business View, promote it and run it from the Work In Progress Window. The result should look like this:

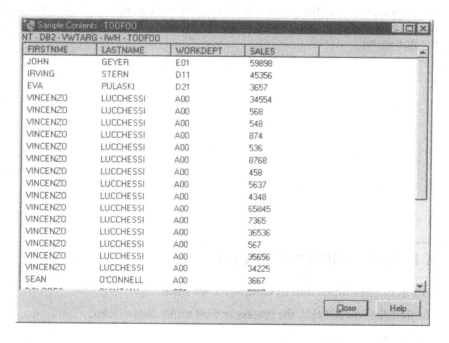

FIRSTNME	LASTNAME	WORKDEPT	SALES
JOHN	GEYER	E01	59898
IRVING	STERN	D11	45356
EVA	PULASKI	D21	3657
VINCENZO	LUCCHESSI	A00	34554
VINCENZO	LUCCHESSI	A00	568
VINCENZO	LUCCHESSI	A00	548
VINCENZO	LUCCHESSI	A00	874
VINCENZO	LUCCHESSI	A00	536
VINCENZO	LUCCHESSI	A00	8768
VINCENZO	LUCCHESSI	A00	458
VINCENZO	LUCCHESSI	A00	5637
VINCENZO	LUCCHESSI	A00	4348
VINCENZO	LUCCHESSI	A00	65845
VINCENZO	LUCCHESSI	A00	7365
VINCENZO	LUCCHESSI	A00	36536
VINCENZO	LUCCHESSI	A00	567
VINCENZO	LUCCHESSI	A00	35656
VINCENZO	LUCCHESSI	A00	34225
SEAN	O'CONNELL	A00	3667

That's it, you have successfully united data from two completely separate sources. Congratulations.

It is worth at this point tracing the steps back to see from where this data comes in practice. 'TooFoo' draws data from two Business Views called 'Foo' and SALES DATA. Consider the Business View 'Foo'. This is connected to a Source which points to the SAMPLE database. However, 'Foo' also has a connection to the table in VWTARG called 'Foo'. It is fair to ask the question "When we run 'TooFoo', it draws data from 'Foo'. 'Foo' has two possible places where it can find the information – the original data, or the table in the data warehouse. Which does it actually consult?".

The answer is...(drum roll)... that it pulls data from the data warehouse not from the Source. In fact, this makes perfect sense and you had probably guessed that anyway, but it just seemed worth making the point explicitly.

Incidentally, we said that you could also get this Business View to give you a view of the data showing the sales totaled for each department. This is left as an exercise for the reader because this is purely an SQL issue and nothing to do with Visual Warehouse. However, out of interest, the figures we got were:

WORKDEPT	Sum Of SALES
A00	240152
D11	65686
E01	59898
D21	17561
C01	3367
E21	648
E11	647

A totally different recap

You may remember that in Chapter 3 we said:

The first time we did this, the process seemed rather longwinded.

- *You create a Source*
- *Then a Warehouse*
- *Next a Business View*
- *Finally you run the Business View*

This led us to pondering why all of the steps were necessary, and by the time you are halfway through, you may be thinking exactly the same. The answer lies in the adaptability of the system that these steps produce.

OK, this is where your hard work is rewarded. It is true that Visual Warehouse has a layout which can seem to border on the pedantic, but that is another way of saying logical, modular and adaptable. This makes it slightly more time consuming to start with, but it does mean that as your data warehouse expands and grows, this expansion is easy to accommodate. As you can see here, plugging in new data is easy.

Potential problems

Just in case we have made this all sound too easy, remember there are a lot of other considerations in this kind of work. The time-consuming elements are likely to be:

- finding out what data is stored and who is in charge of it
- identifying the format of the entries
- determining the cleansing and transforming that's required before the data can be included in the warehouse
- ensuring a path of communication between the hardware/software involved
- agreeing schedules for updating the warehouse data
- keeping everyone happy.

However, these are nothing to do with Visual Warehouse, being more associated with office politics, which can be much harder to drive.

Chapter 10

Security

Security

The good news is that this is going to be a very short chapter, mainly because we assume that you already understand about security in general.

Computing is full of security systems – they appear in networks, databases, mainframes etc. After a while you notice that most (all?) security systems have the same basic elements:

- Objects (which, in turn, have Properties)
- Users
- Logins
- Passwords
- Privileges (a.k.a. Rights)
- Groups

Objects (tables, directories, whatever) have Properties (read, write, alter, delete etc.). Users can be given or denied Privileges to manipulate those Properties.

However, since you may have to deal with multiple Users, it is common for a security system to provide a facility that allows you to put Users into Groups. You can then assign Privileges to Groups, whereupon all of the Users in the Group inherit those Privileges. (*In Visual Warehouse, this is actually the only way of doing it, as you cannot assign Privileges directly to individual Users.*)

In order to protect the system, Users are given a Login which in turn is protected with a Password.

All of this will, we assume, sound familiar to you – in which case the security system in Visual Warehouse will be a piece of cake.

From the Visual Warehouse desktop, pop down the security menu.

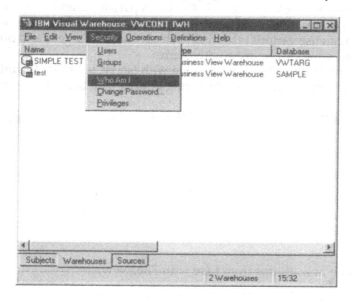

We bet you can't resist the 'Who Am I' option (as if you had forgotten). It should tell you that you are you (you who?)

You can also ask to change your password or to see your Privileges

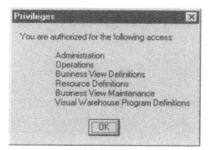

and, because you are the person who installed Visual Warehouse, you should have the full set by default.

If you create new groups, you can assign one or more privileges for that group. While you're learning it's better to keep it simple and assign all privileges to a group. Once you reach the production stage you may wish to limit who can use various resources such as Sources, Targets, and Business Views, and what can be done with them.

Thereafter you can have fun playing with (sorry, learning) the different options. You can have a look at existing groups with Security Groups,

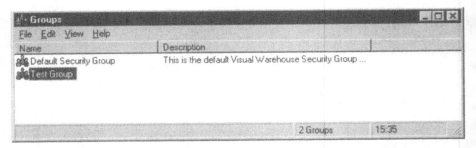

create some new groups from here with File, New,

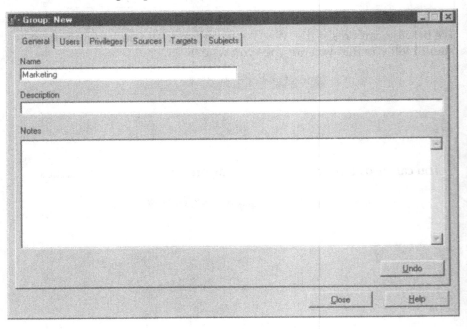

and the different Privileges are explained in the help system

---

Visual Warehouse privileges

A privilege is authorization to perform a particular type of function. You can authorize the users in a security group to one or more of the following types of privileges:

Administration

Allows users to authorize other users to Visual Warehouse by defining user and group definitions, change the Visual Warehouse configuration, and define or edit a subject.

Operations

Allows users to do the following tasks:
- Run, cancel, and purge business views
- View statistics about business view processing
- View information logged about business view processing

Resource Definitions

Allows users to create, update, import, and delete information resources, create and delete warehouses, and modify information resource information in a warehouse definition, and create, update, and delete agent sites.

Business View Definitions

Allows users to create, update, import, and delete business view definitions, change business view status, modify business view information in a warehouse definition, and view the business views contained in a warehouse or subject.

Business View Maintenance

Allows users to modify business views in Production status that have other business views dependent on them. This privilege allows users to demote to Test status Production business views that contribute data to other business views. Once the business view is in Test status, users can add columns to the business view, change the business view's schedule, or move the business view to another warehouse. Users then promote the business view to Production status again.

Attention: Some modifications that the user can make to a business view can cause its dependent business views to fail. We recommend that you grant this status only to those users who are extremely knowledgeable about the business views and their dependencies. The user must promote the business view to Production before the next business view in the tree is scheduled to run, or the scheduled business view will fail.

Program Definitions

Allows users to create, update, import, and delete Program definitions.

The security system is neat, clean and works well.

The only point worth making is that this security system controls the access of users to Visual Warehouse. It does not control the access of users to the data warehouse, since that is stored in DB2 (in our case, in a database called VWTARG). Access to the tables in that database has everything to do with DB2 security and nothing to do with Visual Warehouse.

Chapter 11

DataGuide

DataGuide a.k.a. Visual Warehouse Information Catalog

IBM used to sell a stand-alone product called DataGuide that could be purchased in addition to Visual Warehouse; now the two products are bundled together. During the summer of 1998 it seemed, from IBM presentations and paperwork, as if DataGuide was to be renamed with the snappy title Visual Warehouse Information Catalog. This seemed to us to be accurate but grossly unwieldy. Happily, recent indications are that the original name is to be retained so that is the one we'll use.

So what is DataGuide?

The demonstration data warehouse we have been building so far is so simple that you can hold a picture of what is going on without too much effort. When you move on to a production system several major changes occur.

- The number of objects inside the data warehouse is likely to be much larger.
- Sections of the data warehouse will have been constructed months (or even years) ago and will therefore be less at the forefront of your brain.
- Users of the system won't have your familiarity with the system, so they will find it difficult to navigate through the data warehouse to find the information that they need.
- You, and the users, will eventually want to start associating other objects with the data warehouse.

This last point sounds odd, but it is based on the experience that IBM has had with helping customers to build data warehouses over the years.

These objects can be almost anything, depending on your data warehouse and your company, but common ones might be:

- Documents which describe how the data warehouse works
- People who can and should be contacted for support
- Images
- Presentations
- Comments
- Essentially anything that will help users to make use of the data warehouse.

OK, so production data warehouses are more complex: how does DataGuide help?

DataGuide provides a way of organizing all of the objects. This includes both the objects **within** the data warehouse (tables, fields etc.) and those associated with the data warehouse (documents, etc.)

There is an Administrator section of DataGuide where you can set up and control these objects; there is also a user section where the users can view and use the information.

Two points need to be stressed at this stage.

Firstly, you **don't** have to use DataGuide in order to set up, run, and give users access to, a data warehouse. It simply makes it easier for those users to see the overall structure of the data, and also to see what objects have become associated with the data warehouse.

Secondly, DataGuide is aimed at people building large and complex data warehouses. Given a simple one, you are very unlikely to ever need to use DataGuide. Given a complex data warehouse, experience suggests that you will need something that provides this sort of functionality. And since DataGuide is now bundled with Visual Warehouse (another way of saying that you have already paid for it) you might as well have a look at it in either case.

DataGuide components

DataGuide itself comes in two parts: one is Administrator and the other, User.

The Administrator software comprises tools to perform tasks such as:

- creating an information catalog
- giving users access to the resources they need
- creating "object types" to enable efficient use of information

- imposing a structure on the information catalog to make it easier for users to locate data and to see what's available, by:
  - creating collections of objects
  - grouping objects by their subject
  - making links between objects containing related data
  - adding contact details and comments to objects
  - associating external programs with objects
  - giving users access to further information

The User software provides tools to allow users to browse and search for information resources.

Where do we go from here?

Essentially, DataGuide stores an overview of what is in the data warehouse, together with information about objects associated with the data warehouse. With that in mind, we need to look at two steps.

1. How do we move information about the contents of the data warehouse into DataGuide?
2. How do we add associated objects?

How do we move information about the contents of the data warehouse into DataGuide?

Answer – you, as the DWA, export the metadata (the data that describes the data in the warehouse) from the data warehouse to an information catalog within DataGuide. The users themselves can then use the User version of DataGuide to see what lurks in the data warehouse.

Once a warehouse of tables and business views has been created in Visual Warehouse, the metadata that describes the contents of the warehouse is ready for transfer into the care of DataGuide.

❢ *Everything you enter in Visual Warehouse about sources, targets, tables, columns, business views, schedules, users and so on is held in the control database. Some of this information, but not all, is transferred to DataGuide when you export the metadata.* ❢

Metadata

Metadata from Visual Warehouse must be exported to DataGuide in order for the information catalog to be created. The export process can be automated from within Visual Warehouse so that the Visual Warehouse and DataGuide metadata is synchronized using a scheduled business view to call a program. An example of this type of program is included in the sample data; it's called "VW static metadata synchronization".

We'll illustrate a 'manual' metadata export and then examine what we've achieved.

Getting ready to export to DataGuide

First of all, you must create a database to be used by DataGuide for the exported metadata. This is done from within DB2 just as we did for the control and target databases before installing Visual Warehouse. Our database is DGDATA for obvious reasons and we suggest you use the same name.

Then an 'information catalog' must be prepared to receive data from Visual Warehouse. *Essentially, this information catalog is a collection of nineteen tables in DGDATA that will eventually hold the metadata.* From the Start menu, follow a path through Programs, Visual Warehouse, and DataGuide to Create Information Catalog.

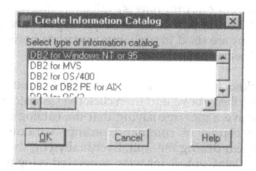

In the first dialog, choose the information catalog type: ours is 'DB2 for Windows NT or 95'. Click OK and you're in the Define Catalog dialog.

The information catalog name is whatever you called the DB2 database you've just created. If the database is held remotely, type in the alias name by which it is know to your workstation.

Next, curiously, you're asked for a 'not-applicable symbol'. The help system says "The not-applicable symbol is the character you enter whenever you don't have the descriptive data for a required item in your information catalog." No, it didn't mean much to us either. Stay tuned, because it will later. For now, accept the default hyphen.

The ID you enter for the 'Primary administrator's user ID' must have SYSADM authority on DB2 so that the administrator can manage the accounts of DataGuide users. Enter the ID of a secondary DataGuide administrator if someone appropriate is available, otherwise leave it blank.

Leave the check box 'Import common object types' checked. These predefined object types are used to exchange metadata between DataGuide and any other software that supports them.

Click Define.

You will be asked for a User ID and password; you can put in the SYSADM one described above and then click the Connect button.

You should receive a message saying that the catalog is being created. Don't worry if a couple of command prompt windows mysteriously appear and disappear during the wait. Eventually you should be told that all is well, and the DataGuide icons were generated; a log file is also identified should you wish to inspect it.

Check out the new icons: there are two of them in the Start, Programs list.

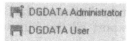

The icons actually represent old-fashioned wooden chest of drawers for storing index cards, such as you may still see in older libraries. On a small scale they don't look like anything much, except maybe, to science fiction film aficionados, those flying porticos in Tron. Anyway, there they both are, icons for DGDATA Administrator and DGDATA User. (DGDATA, you'll remember, is our DB2 database for use with DataGuide).

By all means also have a look at the log file, although this should just be a list of successfully completed operations. You can also, if you want, have a look in DGDATA to see the tables that have been created.

Exporting

From the Visual Warehouse desktop, click File, Export to DataGuide. An Export Warehouse dialog opens.

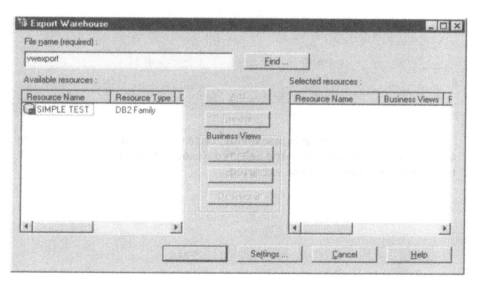

A default name is in place for the file to be exported; you can change this if you want, but it is easier to leave it for now; then your screen will match our screen shots. All available resources (that is, Warehouses) are listed; to select one for export, highlight it and click Add. We'll export SIMPLE TEST.

Beneath the Add and Remove buttons is the Business Views panel. Click the Select All button to export all the business views for the chosen resource, or click Select to pick a subset. (De-select all, not surprisingly, de-selects all business views).

If you click Select, by default business views with test and production status are shown, but you can export views in development too by checking the appropriate box and refreshing the list. (In the main it is likely that a warehouse will be ready for export only once it has passed the development stage, so the default is quite sensible).

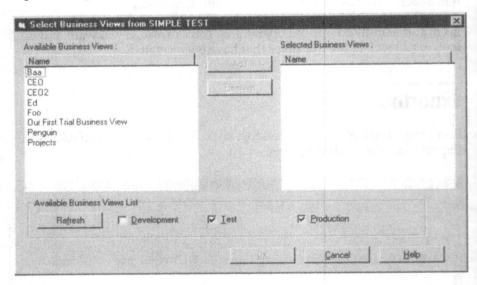

Back in the Export Warehouse dialog, once you've selected the business views, the second column in the Selected Resources list says "Yes" to show that business views are to be exported.

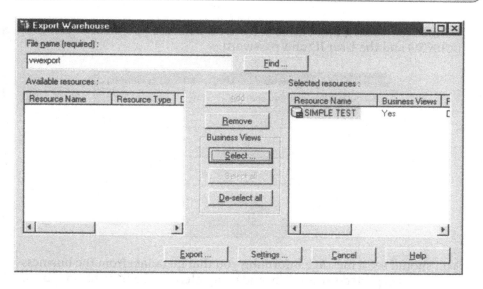

Now click the Settings button to reveal the Export to DataGuide: Settings dialog. There are two decisions to be made: the first is between preserving any name and descriptions that already exist in DataGuide or replacing any existing data. Stick with the default even though the catalog is empty.

The second determines how source tables are mapped to the target warehouse: staying with the default is good here too.

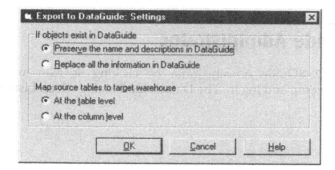

Click OK, and on Export in the Export Warehouse dialog.

Enter the catalog name (this is the DB2 database you created earlier – DGDATA) and the User ID and password.

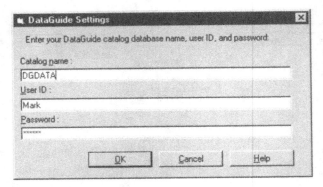

You should see a message informing you that metadata from the business views was exported successfully and completely, and a trace file (a type of log) is identified. Click OK to close this window.

That's it; the metadata has been exported to DataGuide.

❦ *The Export Warehouse function uses lots of CPU time; it won't be an issue with small test exports like the one we've just done, but when you're exporting for real, reduce the system workload, or choose a time when usage is low, before starting the export.* ❧

DataGuide Administrator

Start the DataGuide Administrator by clicking its icon in the Start, Programs menu, and log in. The DataGuide Catalog – Icon List opens.

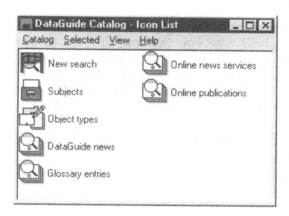

This is the point from which catalog contents are accessed. There are seven icons for reaching various resources; the last four are empty at present. Double click on Subjects; there are two entries in the icon list, one for DB2 Sample Data (the source data defined in Visual Warehouse) and one for SIMPLE TEST (the warehouse).

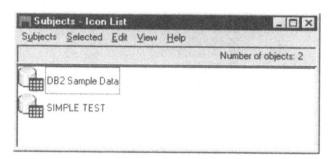

Double click on the warehouse and in the Tree window you see the warehouse and its Business Views are set out in hierarchical fashion. Of course, the Business Views are essentially, when seen from this angle, tables of data with fields. Clicking on the plus symbols, as usual, expands branches of the tree. Expanding each table shows its fields. Right clicking on any object within the tree reveals a host of options, all of which are worth pursuing.

However, the take-home message is clear. You can see the entire system that you have built up. For example, if you choose to examine IWH.PROJECTS, you can see that it contains two fields, DEPTNO and LENGTH. These, in turn, are derived from a table MARK.PROJECT via a transformation (or Business View) called Projects. (LENGTH, if you remember, is calculated from PRENDATE and PRSTDATE).

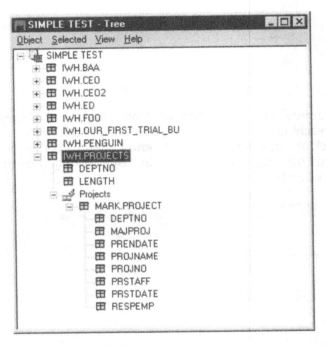

Everything appears to be here, so the metadata export was, indeed, successful. You as a DWA can look at it here, and as you make this information available to users they can see it as well.

How do we add associated objects?

As we said above, the information catalog need not comprise just those tables and business views that are exported as metadata from Visual Warehouse. Many other information resources (objects) can be catalogued within DataGuide.

If you get back to the icon list and double click on the Object types, you can see that DataGuide provides 35 sample object types – audio clips, spreadsheets, presentations, charts etc., each type of which has its own identifying icon.

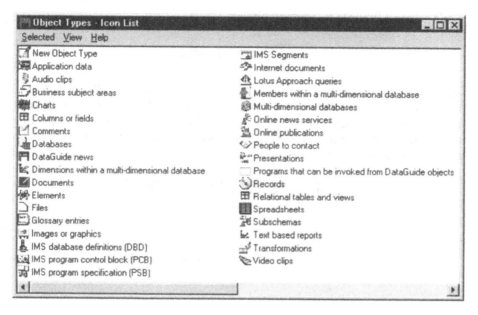

6 *Hint – if you want to use small icons like this, choose the following View options, in the following order.*

>   *View – Small icons*
>   *View – Icons*
>   *View – Icon list*

If you don't, the words associated with the icons tend to become truncated. 9

6 *As an aside, you can also create your own object types to reflect the sorts of business information present in the organization – tables, reports, images, whatever. Each object type can have up to 255 properties to define its characteristics. We'll content ourselves with creating objects which are of a pre-defined type.* 9

Creating an object

Let's create a 'People to contact' object.

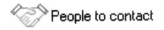 People to contact

Highlight this object type in the object types icon list and click Selected, Create object. (The keyboard shortcut after you've highlighted an object type is Control-J – how memorable). In the Create Object dialog is a list of all the properties for this object type; a cross in the first column means that it's a required property.

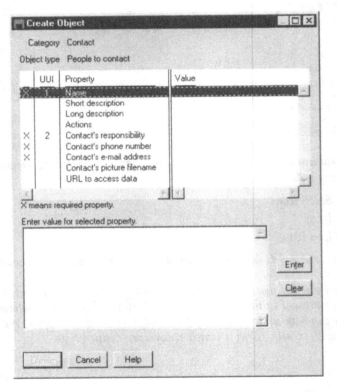

Name is one such, so type a name for the object into the 'Enter value for selected property' box, clicking Enter to move it into the Value column above. Scroll down the list of properties to find other required properties; there are another three for this object type. Enter the contact's responsibility, phone number and email address and, of course, any other information necessary for your overall scheme.

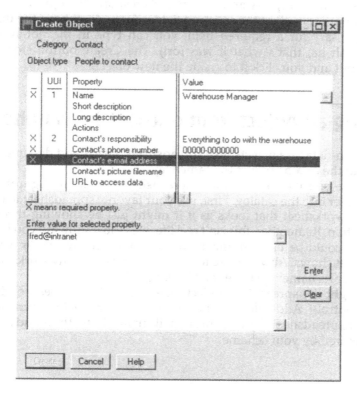

Click OK when you've finished.

Unfortunately, Help is less than helpful when entering values, as it gives no clues about suitable responses: stating the maximum length for a short description, for instance, seemed beyond it. In fact, up to 250 characters are allowed, so 'short' is quite generous. Long descriptions give you up to 32,700 characters to play with and, typically, the limit for the name property is 80 characters.

UUI (Universal Unique Identifier)

The UUI column is, in effect, very like a primary key field. All object types must have at least one UUI property (and can have up to five). The values in these UUIs are used to uniquely identify the objects. Objects of the same name can exist in different catalogs and the UUI prevents such objects from being overwritten when catalogs are combined.

DataGuide's built-in object types have ready-defined UUIs; objects of the 'People to contact' type have a two-part UUI made up of the values for the object name property and the contact's responsibility property.

Make entries in all of the required fields; if you don't have the information necessary for a required field, you can type in the not-applicable symbol (ah ha; that's what it was for!). The Create button stops being grayed out and you click it to create the new object.

Adding an object from outside the warehouse

Other non-database objects (like spreadsheets, charts and documents) are added to the catalog in just the same way.

Imagine you wish to include a spreadsheet containing figures for the first quarter into the catalog. First, use your favorite spreadsheet to create a dummy worksheet that looks as if it might just be showing this sort of information. Remember, this isn't real life, we're just showing you how this software could be used in anger, so it doesn't actually matter what this worksheet shows. All you have to do is to create a dummy worksheet and remember its name: we have called ours Q1.XLS.

Highlight the spreadsheet object type in the object types icon list and press Control-J. Add values to the required property fields; there are only two for a spreadsheet object, name and file name. Enter these and anything else required by your scheme.

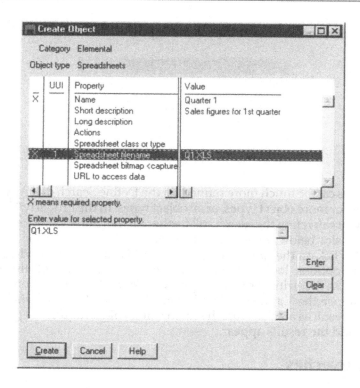

Looking for objects

To check whether the object is present, you must search for it. It seems unwieldy, to say the least, that the only way of seeing what's in the catalog is to instigate a search for it, but that is, indeed, the only way.

Searching

Double click on the New search icon in the icon list, and in the Define Search dialog, select an object type for which to search. We'll look for spreadsheet objects. Move the chosen type by highlighting and using the arrowhead buttons (a double click does not work here).

Click the Search button and the results appear.

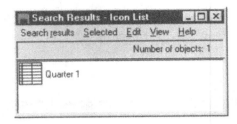

Searches can be much more refined. In the Define Search dialog, you can select one or more object types, or all object types. In the Property/Value list below, you can refine the search still further. In the 'Enter value for selected property' slot below, enter the value for which to search; for example, '*dept*'. Click on the Enter button to place this value in the grid above.

Search options look for the value at the beginning of the string, anywhere in the string, or matching exactly. With the third option you can choose to use the * and ? wildcards. Searching for 'dept' anywhere gives the same result as an exact match search using wildcards for '*dept*'. Click Search, and the results appear.

Saved searches

When you've searched for objects in the information catalog, you can, if you wish, save the search definition for later use. Search definitions appear in the icon list with this icon:

Saved Searches are a great time-saver for frequently-used searches or for ones which are very closely defined.

Help

Your first foray into the help system will show you that it is non-standard Windows NT help – but you'd guessed already that things are somewhat non-standard Windows, hadn't you? The navigation buttons are at the bottom of the window instead of the top, the buttons are labeled differently and searches work differently too. Help cannot be minimized, but will close if you click the Previous button a sufficient number of times to work back through all the pages you've used in the current session. It's not impossible to use, it's just different.

Further organizational controls

There are further levels of organizational control that can be used to build up a catalog to reflect the way data will be accessed by users. For ease of identification, objects can be gathered by subject or into collections.

Categories

This is a classification system for object types. All object types fall into categories, and the category determines how an object type will be handled by DataGuide, defining the actions it can undertake and any relationships between different object types. For example, a Word file containing your organization's mission statement might be an object of the Document type in the Support category (a category for object types that provide additional information about the enterprise or information catalog).

There are seven categories including Grouping (for object types that can themselves contain object types) and Attachment (for object types for attaching information, such as a comment, to another object).

Subjects

A Grouping category object can be used to store objects concerned with the same subject area. A single Grouping can contain other groupings, and you can use these to build up a hierarchy to reflect data flow within the organization. For instance, a sales figures grouping can contain a grouping for home and export sales figures, and each of those can contain groupings for retail, wholesale and discounted sales figures.

Collections

A collection is a container for objects. Objects that are likely to be used by a single user or a group of users can be kept together in a collection, even though they may span different subject areas.

Links between objects

It is possible to put in place links between objects containing related data, making such relationships easier to trace.

Contact details

Objects can have contact details associated with them; ideally these would be up-to-date details of the right person to contact in the event of any queries or problems.

Comments

Comments are like those yellow sticky notes attached to objects: they're quick to attach and delete and are very useful as reminders or notes on possible improvements. Comments are often temporary, being discarded once acted upon.

Invoking programs from DataGuide objects

External applications can be associated with objects, so that Word can be launched to read a document, for instance. There are 24 pre-defined objects of the type "Programs that can be invoked from DataGuide objects".

All the usual housekeeping tasks can be carried out with DataGuide; tasks like copying, updating, the general organization of objects into the relevant hierarchy and collections, and the definition of new object types.

A few other snippets

Tag language

All the tasks performed from the GUI can also be undertaken using the tag language. The foregoing sentence is for information only; we wouldn't recommend you delve into this unless it's absolutely vital. The tag language is at its most useful for performing tasks in bulk or for a form of backup: Visual Warehouse metadata can be exported to tag files that can then be backed up; however it's perfectly acceptable and easier to back up using DB2. Only the largest catalogs will require knowledge of tag language, so cross it off your list of things to worry about for now.

Web interface

A Web interface to DataGuide can be installed, allowing users to access the catalog from their chosen browser software.

Summary

DataGuide is a great organizational tool, but as with all tools, it is only truly useful if you need it. If your warehouse isn't huge and your data not particularly complex, you don't need it. The comfort is that you know it's there if you ever do.

Chapter 12

Overview of Visual Warehouse components

This chapter contains no practical work. Instead it provides an overview of the components that make up Visual Warehouse so that, when you deploy them in anger, you will have more of an idea of how they should be used.

Visual Warehouse components

Visual Warehouse is composed of three main parts. These are the Visual Warehouse Manager, the Visual Warehouse Agent and the Visual Warehouse Administrative Client.

Visual Warehouse Manager

When you install Visual Warehouse, you acquire the services of a Manager. It has control over everything that happens. It scans the control database for Business Views to be run, and when one is ready to run, the manager obtains details including the source, target, any SQL code and/or program name and the Agent site (see below) for the Business View and passes that information to the appropriate agent site. It awaits the agent's report on the successful completion (or failure) of the Business View, and then updates the control database accordingly, placing records as appropriate in the WIP window, Statistics and Log files.

Visual Warehouse Agent

An agent is a piece of software that sits between a data source and Visual Warehouse Manager, and it is under the control of the manager. An agent's tasks are to transfer data between the source and the warehouse, and to run Visual Warehouse programs. The description of each task it carries out is held in a Business View.

Agents come in various flavors to suit various operating systems; we're using the NT agent, but others available include OS/2 and AIX, with AS/400 coming soon.

You can (within broad limits) have any number of agents you like, and an agent can move data from any source to any target. One agent can write to many targets, and many agents can write to one target.

An agent can sit in several locations, but for the best performance, ideally it should be placed on the target machine. If your server is a powerful one, that server can run happily with the manager and the agent installed. An agent installed on the server is called a local agent. This approach is commonly adopted; in IBM's experience, the agent sits on the Visual Warehouse server in over 50% of cases. You can also run the manager on the Visual Warehouse server and store the target database and the agent on another, the agent is then termed a remote agent.

Agents do not require to be set up with access to the control database as they do not communicate directly with it; all such communication is channeled through the manager.

Agent Site

An Agent Site is simply a machine on which the Visual Warehouse Agent code is installed, and which is registered as an agent site with Visual Warehouse Manager. Any computer that is to act as an agent site must have TCP/IP installed to enable it to communicate with the Visual Warehouse server.

Visual Warehouse Administration Client

The Administration Client is the GUI, and all the windows you ever see come from here. The manager and agent software have no GUI component.

The GUI has to run on Windows NT, and can sit on the same machine as the manager and the agent, or on a machine with one of them or with neither of them (i.e. on its own in splendid isolation). You can have any number of Administration Clients (with no overhead), and an Administration Client can control a number of Visual Warehouse Managers.

The Administration Client must have access to the control database to enable it to write into the database everything that's entered through the GUI.

Data Warehouse Administrator

There is, of course, another vital element in a Visual Warehouse implementation, and that's the Administrator, the hard-working, under-appreciated human being whose job it is to keep all the balls in the air at once and all the time.

The responsibilities of a DWA

There follows a list of the tasks and responsibilities that fall to the lot of the DWA. It's a long list, some items being one-off or infrequent tasks and some needing attention on a day-to-day basis.

- Creating security groups and assigning privileges to those groups
- Registering users with Visual Warehouse and assigning them to groups
- Other security issues (new passwords etc.)
- Registering Sources with Visual Warehouse
- Registering Warehouses with Visual Warehouse
- Creating Subjects within Visual Warehouse
- Registering Visual Warehouse Programs with Visual Warehouse
- Registering Agents with Visual Warehouse
- Creating/Maintaining/Running Business Views
- Monitoring WIP on a regular basis and taking action as required
- Running Business Views on request
- Monitoring Visual Warehouse logs and statistics
- Creating DataGuide catalogs
- Exporting metadata to DataGuide
- Exporting Visual Warehouse metadata to tag files for backup, to load on other Visual Warehouse systems or for documentation purposes.

Chapter 13

OLAP concepts and terminology

OK, we admit it. This chapter is another theoretical one, just like Chapter 12. It covers concepts like OLAP, dimensions (sparse and dense), members and hierarchies. If these are meat and drink to you, feel free to skip to Chapter 14. If not, we recommend that you read this chapter first.

OLAP concepts and terminology

OLAP is wonderful, it's great, we love it – you can tell there is a 'but' coming, can't you? – but it has developed some rather odd terminology already (and the field is still young). In fairness, it also has some rather unusual concepts as well so it needs new terminology to describe these.

We think it's worth getting your brain around the concepts and terminology first, before trying to get the software to function. Otherwise you end up trying to learn the concepts, the terminology and how to drive the software all at the same time. Some people can manage this trick but we can't. So, without further ado, here's an introduction to the concepts and terminology of OLAP.

What does OLAP mean?

OLAP stands for On-Line Analytical Processing. DB2 OLAP Server is the software that manipulates the data, and the data manipulated by DB2 OLAP Server is stored in an OLAP cube. (The term **cube** reflects the multi-dimensional aspects of data storage, though it could just as easily be called a database).

❛ *We think that OLAP can be a rather misleading term. The 'On-Line' bit could be taken to imply that the data is on-line in the sense that people are still updating it; in other words, implying that the data is available for interactive use. In fact, OLAP uses a copy of this operational data in the same way that a data warehouse does. (The data is structured very differently in an OLAP cube, so in other ways the two copies are very different). The 'On-Line' in OLAP refers to the fact that OLAP offers users of the system the ability to analyze the data in real-time. They can ask to see the data in a particular way and the answer should come back in seconds rather than in days.* ❜

So, having defined OLAP, are we any nearer to understanding it? Not really, no. OK, let's try another tack.

You are the manager of a large retail chain. Every store collects data about sales and sends it to corporate headquarters where it is all consolidated. It is your job to make sense of the data. You want to look for trends – does Wuffles dog food sell better on the West coast than on the East? Are sales in Europe increasing or decreasing? Do the French preferentially buy French wine? Do people in Seattle really buy more expensive coffee?

In order to answer this last question, you have to sift through huge sets of figures. You have to find all of the stores that are within the Seattle area and average their coffee sales for each brand. Then you have to do the same for the rest of the US. Finally, after hours or even days, you can compare the figures. Ah, it's true! Seattalites do spend more on quality coffee! But that leads to the thought "Does that mean they spend less on tea?" Back to the figures....

There must be an easier way. There is; it's called OLAP.

As we said, we don't really like the term OLAP and prefer the broader term Multi-Dimensional Analysis (MDA). This seems more appropriate since data can be considered to have dimensions and all we do with OLAP is to manipulate data within these dimensions. OLAP makes extensive use of dimensions, so let's have a look at those.

Dimensions and members

Imagine, if you will, that you suddenly decide to give up computing and go into retailing. You open a small shop and start selling goods – pumpkins, artichokes, haddock, herring, halibut and hake. (There is no significance in the fact that all of the fish begin with h).

You note down the number of items sold every day, and after a week you have a table of data (to stop the table becoming too wide, we've been politically incorrect and displayed the dates in non Y2K compliant format.)

Date	1/1/99	1/2/99	1/3/99	1/4/99	1/5/99	1/6/99	1/7/99
Pumpkin	2	3	0	0	1	2	1
Artichoke	4	2	2	0	0	6	0
Haddock	3	0	0	2	8	3	2
Herring	0	1	1	6	10	4	2
Halibut	1	2	0	1	2	3	1
Hake	2	3	0	4	0	2	1

Now, in OLAP terminology, you have two **dimensions** here. For the sake of argument we can call these dimensions 'Time' and 'Products'. Each dimension has a number of **members** – Time currently has seven members and Products has six. There are, therefore, 7 * 6 = 42 possible intersections between members of the two dimensions. Each of these intersections has a value (even if it is a zero).

So far, so easy.

At the end of a month's trading you have a larger table. Time now has, say, 30 members and so there are now 180 intersections. Having collected all of this data, you want to ask some questions about how your trade is going. You may well want to know things like:

- the total number of items sold
- the total number of each product sold
- the total sold for each day

and so on.

These are easy to work out: you just have to total the rows and columns. (Very spreadsheety, this.)

However, you may want to perform slightly more complex analyses such as how many items you sold in each week. This might, in turn, lead you to become interested in the sales of haddock week by week.

Then you might want to know how fish is selling in comparison to vegetables. In other words, it is very common for people who look at data in this way to want to 'group' the members of a dimension in a variety of ways. Here the individual members in the Products dimension have been grouped into sales of vegetables and fish by week.

	Week 1	Week 2	Week 3	Week 4
Vegetables	23	18	34	65
Fish	64	53	45	43

Developing a hierarchy

As the number of members increases, it is also common for users to want/require a hierarchy of groupings. You might want the days in the Time dimension to be grouped into weeks, then into months, then quarters and finally years. At present you might want the products to be grouped into fish and vegetables, but as you add products you may also want to add groups and a hierarchical structure. For instance, food might embrace both fish and vegetables, while clothing could embrace jeans and shoes.

In OLAP terminology, Haddock is described as a 'member' of the dimension Products. '1/1/1999' is also a member, but of the dimension Time. In fact, both of these are **'leaf node** members'. Why? Well, we have so far used the rather nebulous term 'grouping' to describe the aggregations of members (such as Week and Fish). In correct OLAP parlance, these are also called members. Thus Haddock, Herring, Week, Quarter 1 and Fish are all members of their respective dimensions. The term leaf node refers to those at the bottom of the hierarchy – such as Haddock and '1/1/99'; that is, the ones that cannot be sub-divided. The others (such as Fish and Week) are simply called 'members' or 'higher members'.

It is worth remembering the term leaf node, because it will surface again at the end of this chapter.

What about more dimensions?

Dimensions are only added as and when required. For example, if your store is successful, you might open another store in a different town. Soon you have two sets of data and that means you have acquired another dimension. Then you open a third store, a fourth and a fifth. Now you find that you want to do the 'grouping' thing again because stores are located in cities, cites in states, states in countries and so on. You are also likely to want to summarize some of the data by these 'categories'.

❝ *Incidentally, there is a temptation to call this dimension something like Stores, but once you consider the other members that you might add (cities, states, countries etc.) a broader name like Geography or Location is often more appropriate. Of course, there are no absolute rules here, you can call the dimensions and members whatever you like; it's up to you.* ❞

Some dimensions will have only a few members – a dimension might only hold members for projected sales and actual sales, for example. Others, like Time, are likely to have a large number of members.

A cubic perspective

When you query an OLAP cube of data, any value you request must relate to a member from each dimension. Whether you want to know the fish sales in March for Boston, or the years' artichoke sales in Seattle, or the first quarter vegetable sales everywhere, you have a value which combines data from all three dimensions. Data from the intersections of any member from any level in any dimension can be accessed rapidly to give you an answer.

The database grows...

It should be obvious that when you add another dimension, you dramatically increase the number of intersections. Given a year's worth of data and 20 products you will have approximately 300 * 20 = 6,000 intersections. If you have 25 stores, you have 300 * 20 * 25 = 150,000 (or more; see Chapter 19). Add another dimension, say sales people, of whom you have 100 and the number leaps to 15 million. Even if you add a dimension with only two members, you double the number of intersections. This means that it is easy for OLAP cubes to become very large very rapidly.

Sparse and dense dimensions

However, it is worth noting that not all intersections are the same. When we started with this example, we used Time and Products as the two dimensions. We said for those dimensions that all the intersections would contain a value, even if it was zero.

Now consider the interaction of two very simple dimensions, People and Stores. We'll assume for the moment that they have no complex hierarchy of members (so it's OK to use the name Stores rather than Geography). You have 25 stores and four staff at each store. That makes 100 people in all. So the People dimension has 100 members and the Stores one has 25. Thus the number of intersections between the Store dimension and the People dimension is 25 * 100 = 2,500. But you've probably already spotted the logical flaw here. For each sales person, we have the ability to record the sales that they make at every single store. Yet Jim works in Boston; he never has, and he never will, make a sale in Seattle. This means that 24 out of 25 Store/People intersections are going to be wasted or put another way, 96% of these intersections are going to be wasted. Wasted in this sense means that, as intelligent human beings, it is apparent to us that these intersections are never going to be used.

Is this simply interesting, or is it something that should concern you? The answer is that you really do need to be aware of this problem. Data cubes grow at an alarming rate without us making the problem worse by asking them to set aside massive amounts of storage space that will never be used. So, what can we do about it?

At this point two more OLAP terms appear on the scene to save the day. They are **sparse** and **dense** and are applied to dimensions; you can have **sparse dimensions** and **dense dimensions**.

In a nutshell, a sparse dimension is one where there are values for a low percentage of possible data positions (i.e. intersections where meaningful values will be stored), and a dense dimension has values for a high percentage of possible data positions.

In the scenario above, People and Stores are sparse dimensions: as discussed, there will never be any data for Jim's sales in Seattle (sale-less in Seattle?).

Time, however, is a classically dense dimension; time rolls on relentlessly and data is collected remorselessly. Regardless of what you sell where, it is probable that you will have data for every day, month, quarter and year that you're in business. (OK, so you may not open your stores at the weekend, but then you don't record those days in the database.) The Time dimension is, therefore, identified as dense in almost every case.

The good news is that, as long as you can identify the sparse and dense dimensions, you can tell DB2 OLAP Server which is which. In return, DB2 OLAP Server will modify the way that it stores them in the cube which dramatically reduces the size of the cube and speeds up the process of returning answers.

Data collection

It is important to realize that, in both this hypothetical example and in real life, what you collect is raw data. You don't collect weekly totals, you don't collect quarterly totals; you collect the sort of data that fits in at the leaf node level of the hierarchy.

Why is this so important?

It means that you are going to have to understand both the raw data that you collect and the way in which you want it to be organized before you start

Let's have a look at an example.

As we said before, your business has been successful. By the year 2000 you have 25 stores using 100 sales people to sell 20 different products. We'll assume that you never have more than one store per city. At the end of that year you have collected, say, 300 days worth of data. You are thinking about setting up an OLAP cube to analyze the data, but you haven't actually done anything yet.

You consider the data that you've collected and the analysis that you want to do. It occurs to you that you have essentially four dimensions:

Time
Geography
People
Products

You decide that you will want to 'group' information within these dimensions like this:

Time	Products
Year	Product Type (Vegetable or Fish)
Quarter	Product
Month	
Day	

Geography	People
Country	
State	
Store	

So, you have decided upon the dimensions and members that you're going to need. Note that People doesn't have any hierarchy. That's fine, members within dimensions are not obligatory; only use them if to do so suits you.

Now you look at the data that you have actually collected. This will hopefully be in a properly normalized relational database. However, it should be a relatively trivial task to query that database and produce an answer table that looks like this:

Store	Date	Person	Product	Number
Seattle	1/1/2000	Sally	Pumpkin	0
Seattle	1/1/2000	Sally	Artichoke	1
Boston	1/1/2000	Jim	Pumpkin	1
Seattle	1/1/2000	Fred	Haddock	4

and so on. Given what we have said about sparse and dense data, in theory you could have 25 * 100 * 20 = 50,000 rows for each date. In practice, no one in their right minds will have collected that 'sparse' data, so your table will have more like 25 * 4 * 20 = 2,000 rows per date, say 300 * 2,000 = 600,000 rows for the year.

So, you have your hierarchies planned on paper and you have the raw data. How do you put the two together?

Well, think of it this way. Suppose that you tell DB2 OLAP Server that you want a new cube and that it is to have four dimensions called Time, Geography, People and Products. Now, suppose that you concentrate on Time. You tell DB2 OLAP Server that:

A year consists of 4 quarters Q1, Q2, Q3 and Q4

Q1 consists of Jan, Feb, March

Q2 consists of April, May, and June, etc.

Then you tell it that:

Jan consists of 1/1/2000 up to and including 1/31/2000

Feb is... and so on,

and that:

The US is a country.

Washington is a state in the US

Seattle is a city in Washington, etc.

This sounds a little tedious, but there are ways of automating the process. The important point is that if you give DB2 OLAP Server all of this information, then it has enough to do something very intelligent.

If you feed it this raw data:

Store	Date	Person	Product	Number
Seattle	1/1/2000	Sally	Pumpkin	0
Seattle	1/1/2000	Sally	Artichoke	1
Boston	1/1/2000	Jim	Pumpkin	1
Seattle	1/1/2000	Fred	Haddock	4
and so on for another 600,000 or so rows.				

it will be able to put all of this data into its correct place within the structure. Take the first row. This row doesn't directly tell DB2 OLAP Server that this belongs to the member Washington, and to the member Q1 and also to the member Vegetable. However, when you defined the structure of the cube you gave DB2 OLAP Server the vital information that Seattle is in Washington, a Pumpkin is a vegetable etc. so it can make the deduction for itself.

Something else you will have done when you defined the structure of the cube is to have told DB2 OLAP Server what to do with the data between levels. Thus you will have told it to sum the values for each day to produce a value for the month, and to sum the appropriate values for each quarter and so on.

Once the raw data has been loaded into the OLAP cube, you can tell DB2 OLAP Server to calculate all of the missing values (those for the higher level members) and it will be able to do so. We said earlier that the leaf nodes were important. It should now be apparent that a good way of expressing what is typically done is to load the cube with leaf node data. You rarely give it data from the higher levels (such as Fish) because DB2 OLAP Server will calculate the data that need to go there.

❛ *Of course, DB2 OLAP server is very versatile. If you happen to have the data that can be loaded into the higher levels, it is perfectly possible to load it into the OLAP cube.* ❜

Summary

You have a mass of raw data and you want to analyze it in a multi-dimensional way.

1. You identify the dimensions and the groups into which you want data to be organized.
2. You use DB2 OLAP Server to build an OLAP cube and define the dimensions, the members and the relationships between the members.
3. You query your operational database and produce a table (which could be a simple text file) that contains all of the leaf node data.
4. You load that data into the OLAP cube.
5. You tell DB2 OLAP Server to calculate the data for the higher level members in the cube.

The next three chapters will get you to the point where you really can do all of this, and with your own data too.

Chapter 14

Installing DB2 OLAP Server

Setting the scene

DB2 OLAP Server is a tool that enables you to build and manipulate multi-dimensional cubes of data. You can think of the product as having several layers:

- the end user client element comprising:
  - the Application Manager, for defining and managing data cubes
  - the Spreadsheet Interface and/or other client tools, used to access and manipulate data
- the OLAP engine – the server component
- the storage mechanism for the cube of data – the relational database.

These definitions can be expanded:

- The Application Manager is essentially the user interface you'll use to drive DB2 OLAP server.
- The OLAP engine is the bit of code that actually processes requests for information, understands about sparse and dense dimensions, security etc.
- The cube of data is actually held as tables in a DB2 database. Thus, in order to run DB2 OLAP Server, you need to have DB2 installed and running on the same machine. (There's also another layer, the Relational Storage Manager, that sits between DB2 and the OLAP engine but that is essentially transparent.)

Various add-on features are also available (SQL Interface, Partitioning option, Web Gateway, Spreadsheet Toolkit, etc.) should your implementation require the added functionality they offer.

The only complication to this story lies in the naming. The Application Manager and the OLAP engine are provided by a product called Essbase, and was originally supplied to IBM by a company called Arbor Software.

Following a company merge (like a mail merge only different) Essbase is now supplied by Hyperion Solutions.

We mention this only because, depending upon what documentation you have, you may well see any of these three names (Essbase, Arbor, Hyperion) at different times. It doesn't really matter; IBM supplied the product to you and takes full responsibility for the three components that make up DB2 OLAP Server.

Before starting to install DB2 OLAP Server

Fire up DB2 and create a DB2 database, just as you did before installing Visual Warehouse. This is where the multi dimensional data will be stored; we called our database DB2OLAP and strongly recommend that you do the same so that your work matches the screen shots in the book.

For performance reasons on a production system we'd recommended that you use DMS (database managed space) table space instead of SMS (system managed space); for a first trial run it's unlikely to be critical so you can stick with the SMS defaults for the time being.

It is a good idea to have the following pieces of information on hand; you'll be asked for them during installation:

- The name of the database you've just created (DB2OLAP)
- The DB2 user ID and password you used to create it (we use our standard persona, as described in the introduction)

You'll also be asked for the table space name you want DB2 OLAP Server to use but it's not required information. If you know it, that's fine, but don't worry if you don't.

Make sure you know exactly what you have bought as you'll be asked to identify the tools and modules that should be installed from the CD-ROM.

It's also wise to check that the latest Windows NT & DB2/UDB (Universal DataBase) service/fix packs have been applied.

On the DB2 OLAP Server CD-ROM you should find a file called Readme.txt. There is a lot of information in here, including some installation notes that might be relevant to your system, so a quick browse of this file could be useful. You'll be seeing it automatically after the installation is complete, which is rather late in the day for installation tips!

It's phooey time again. The memory requirement for DB2 OLAP Server running under NT is given as "64Mb or more". Right. We'll take the "or more" option, thank you; 256Mb is better.

❦ *We were told by the guys at IBM that it has been known (albeit rarely) for the path to become corrupted during a DB2 OLAP Server installation, though we did not experience this during the many installations we ran. However, as a precaution before you start the installation, copy and paste the PATH (found on the Environment tab in Control Panel, System) into a text file and keep it somewhere safe as a backup if things do go wrong.*

Installation

Point to the CD-ROM with Windows Explorer and run Setup.exe. The first window is concerned with the license agreement, and then we're into the installation proper.

Select the products you wish to install, clicking to the left of each to select or de-select them. As a general rule, don't chose more than you need. For example, if you are using 32 bit Excel, don't select the Add-in for Excel 5.0. We'll be using Excel 97 and have selected the Client products as shown below. We also selected all of the Server product options.

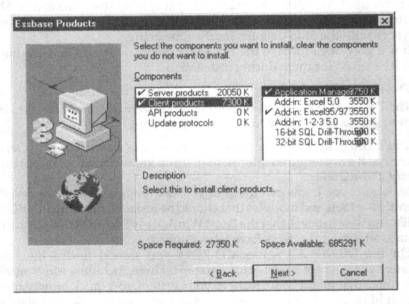

Almost all of the installation process is straightforward and the default settings are fine.

- For questions about network protocols, specific knowledge of your system might lead you to choose something other than the default.
- By default you'll install the on-line HTML help which is recommended.

- The dialog that asks if you want the environment settings updated automatically is the exception. The default is No but we think you should answer Yes unless you really know of a good reason not to do so.

You work your way through the dialogs and a command prompt window opens, running License.exe. This is where you must specify the components to install: the selection shown below is a random selection just to give you the idea but clearly you must only select the options that have been purchased!

```
C:\TEMP\_1STMP3.DIR\license.exe                              _ □ ×
y

Did you purchase the Web Gateway? (Y/N)
n

Did you purchase the Adjustment Module? (Y/N)
n

Your responses are summarized below.

Quantity Description
       1  Workgroup Edition    1.0
       0  Additional Concurrent Users
       0  Partitioning Option 1.0
       1  Tools Bundle         1.0
       1  Objects              1.0
       0  Web Gateway          1.0
       0  Adjustment Module    1.0

Are you satisfied with this allocation of options to this server? (Y/N)
If you respond with "Y", these choices will be recorded in
LICENSE.LOG and DB2 OLAP Server will be enabled to use the
indicated options.  If you respond with "N", your previous
responses will be discarded and you will be prompted again.
```

A dialog will ask for information to update the RSM.CFG file (see below). Type in the name of the DB2 database you've just created, together with the user ID and password that you used in DB2 when you created that database – but beware! This dialog is a trap for the unwary in several ways. Firstly, it will show your password in plain text, so make sure no one is looking over your shoulder who shouldn't see it.

Secondly, you may find that, for some unfathomable reason, each field contains a leading space character. You must delete these spaces, otherwise the details you enter may be stored incorrectly. (*This was true for version 3.1 and the beta of 5.2. If you really **can't** find these spaces, they may have been removed from the final version of 5.2.*)

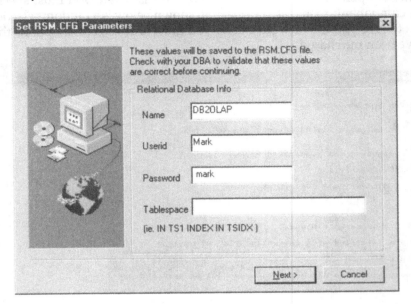

This screen shot shows the problem in the password field. The leading space is still there, so don't use this screen as a role model. (Also, before anyone jumps on us, we never really use the same string for ID and password. But, much as we love you, we aren't going to reveal the real password we use...)

The selected products are now installed; they're identified in the top left of the screen and the usual progress bars are shown. When all is in place, you're shown the Read.me file, and then you must re-boot the machine.

Starting Essbase for the first time

Open a command prompt window and breath deeply; there'll be a GUI along in a minute. At the prompt type

```
essbase
```

6 *As explained above, DB2 OLAP Server uses the Essbase OLAP engine, and that's what you're starting up here.* 9

You are asked for several pieces of information. The first is a company name to embed into the server license registration.

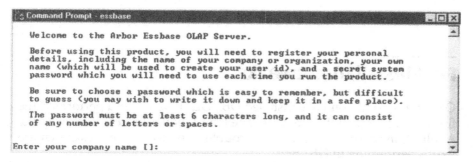

The next item is requested with the words "Enter your name", a choice of phrase open to much misinterpretation. This "name" will, in fact, be the name you use as the user ID for Essbase; again we recommend that you use the same ID and password that you have been using all along. Note that the password will be shown on screen, so be careful.

Once you have verified your entries, the DB2 OLAP Server starts and presents this message showing it's ready to rock and roll:

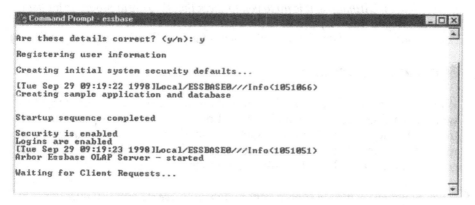

The next time you start DB2 OLAP Server, you'll only have to supply the password.

Stopping Essbase

You don't necessarily have to do this yet, but when you do want to stop the server you simply return to this command window and type

```
quit
```

at the prompt.

Post-installation tweaks

OK, at this point you have installed DB2 OLAP Server and performed the first start up of the OLAP engine. The temptation is to rush into using the Application Manager but there's a couple of housekeeping tasks that are worth performing in DB2 first.

Remember that DB2 OLAP Server runs on top of DB2, storing its data in a DB2 database. If you try to do this with a copy of DB2 that's running with default settings, things are likely to get nasty. This isn't really IBM's fault. DB2 isn't configured, by default, to run as the back-end for DB2 OLAP Server so some tweaking is to be expected.

❛ *The figures that we quote below were gleaned from the manuals and also from the IBMers at Santa Teresa and Warwick. We can, however, only offer a set of 'get you going' figures. Ultimately, it is up to you to check that they are appropriate for your system. As you gain experience with your system, feel free to make whatever changes seem appropriate. This is another way of saying "Your mileage may vary".* ❜

Transaction handling

When you start loading and calculating data, as you will in Chapter 15, DB2 will record these actions in its log files. Load and calculate operations are treated by default as single transactions, so if the database is large (and multi-dimensional databases are renowned for their size) the logs will contain many records and require many files.

❛ *If you're not familiar with transactions and logging, we'll point you once again to 'DB2 for Windows NT – Fast', mentioned in the introduction.* ❜

There are two approaches to this, and the simple one is to increase the size and number of log files. Clearly the changes that you make will depend upon the size of your cube, but the following figures are from

IBMers with considerable experience so they should be OK to at least get you started.

- The default log file size is 250 * 4k pages. Expand this to something like 1,000 or 2,500 * 4k pages.
- The default numbers of log files are three primary and two secondary log files. Increase the number of secondary log files to perhaps100.

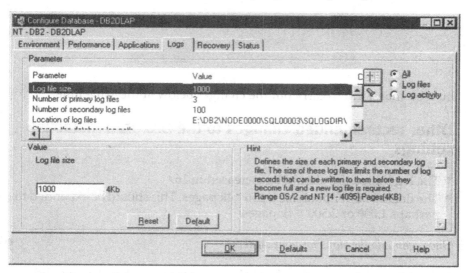

6 *Note that these two changes considerably increase the amount of disk space that the log files can potentially request from the system. If each log file is 1000 * 4K it occupies 4 Mbytes. There will be three primary log files during normal running, so that's 12 Mbytes. The secondary log files aren't always used, but if all 100 were actually to be used, they would occupy 1.2 Gbytes. Make sure you have that spare capacity!* **9**

Both these parameters are found by right clicking on the database in DB2's Control Center, selecting Configure and going to the Logs tab. Note that you are simply altering these parameters for the DB2OLAP database, not for the complete DB2 instance.

If you click on the OK button, you'll be given instructions about restarting

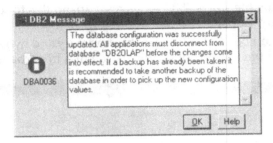

but you may want to carry out the changes below at the same time.

Other recommended changes to the DB2OLAP database settings

- The log buffer size should be increased to 16.
- The default buffer pool size is 250 * 4k pages. This should be expanded to perhaps 1,000 or 2,500 * 4k pages.

❝ *Once again, do the sums for your system.* ❞

- The application heap size should be increased to 1024, just as you did for Visual Warehouse.

All these parameters are found as before but on the Performance tab.

An alternative approach to transaction handling

Apart from increasing the log file size and number of secondary logs for the DB2 database, you can (as recommended in the IBM documentation) set the Essbase Commit Block parameter to a specific number of blocks.

This parameter is found as follows. In the Application Manager (which will be introduced more fully in Chapter 15), highlight a database and then direct your attention to the Transaction tab in the dialog found under Database, Settings in the Application Manager menu.

The manual says that the default is 3000. In the pre-release version of DB2 OLAP Server 1.0.1, the Commit Block parameter was set to zero, but it's possible that this may change in the release version.

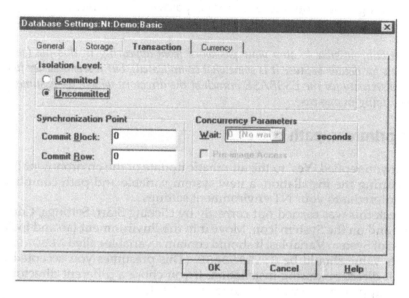

Either way, we are reaching realms of fine tuning which are beyond the scope of this book. Valid choices depend entirely on the circumstances that pertain to your system, and we direct you to the Essbase documentation. We only mention this parameter because it appears in the documentation and you may well need to find it at some stage.

Troubleshooting

We can't do much in a book this size, but here are two places to look if all is not well.

DB2 connect statement

The DB2 connections use the database name, user ID and password you specified during installation. This information is placed in a file called RSM.CFG which is the configuration file for the Relational Storage Manager, the software that sits between DB2 and the Essbase OLAP engine.

You can look at its contents by locating the RSM.CFG file in C:\
ESSBASE\BIN using Windows Explorer and double clicking on it. If necessary, choose a tool with which to view it (Notepad is fine). It shows your
DB2 settings and, you'll also find your password is stored there in plain
text.

❻ *It's actually possible to stop your password from appearing in this file (see the*
manuals for details because it is somewhat complicated), but it seems easier just to
enforce security for the ESSBASE branch of the directory which, we assume, you
will be doing in any case. ❾

The primrose path

When you replied 'Yes' to the automatic update of the environment question during the installation, a new system variable and path component
was entered into your NT environment settings.

Check this was carried out correctly by clicking Start, Settings, Control
Panel and on the System icon. Move into the Environment tab and look in
the list of System Variables. It should contain a variable called ARBORPATH,
and its value should be C:\ESSBASE. (This presumes you accepted the
default directory during installation. If you chose a different directory, it
should appear as the variable alongside ARBORPATH).

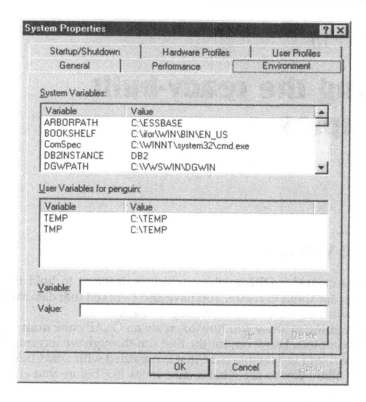

An addition is made to the end of the PATH statement too, so that its final portion reads:

```
C:\ESSBASE\BIN
```

Progress

You've installed the software, made tweaks to DB2 as you see fit and completed the initiation of your copy of DB2 OLAP Server. You may wish to stop and restart NT at this point to ensure that all of the changes are in effect.

Chapter 15

Using the ready-built samples

Where you are

You have created a DB2 database which is destined to hold the OLAP cubes you are about to create. You have also tweaked that database so that it is better suited to holding such cubes of data.

We are going to show you how to create an OLAP cube from scratch in the later chapters. However, for the first run through we recommend that you make use of the sample cube that is provided with DB2 OLAP Server. This will allow you to see what a cube looks like before you create your own.

Creating the samples

The act of installing DB2 OLAP Server should have copied the files necessary to create the sample cube onto your hard disk. Check this out using Explorer by going to the directory

```
c:\essbase\bin
```

and looking for a file called `sample.exe`.

The file is (hopefully) there and running that file will cause the sample cube to be created. But first you must start Essbase.

Starting Essbase

Open a command prompt window (sorry) and type 'essbase' at the prompt.

You're asked for the system password – this is the one you entered during installation. Type it in.

❛ *Late breaking news tells us that with version 1.0.1 it will be possible to register DB2 OLAP Server as an NT service. Details of how to do this are yet to be released, but it's something worth investigating.* ❜

Lines appear to tell you that the startup sequence is complete, that security and logins are enabled and that Hyperion Essbase OLAP Server is started. It also says Waiting for Client Requests...

Despite this message that gives a kind of 'left hanging on the telephone' feeling, you have indeed started Essbase successfully. Don't close the window, although you can minimize it to clear some screen space.

❛ *Other command prompt windows are going to be used during this chapter and it is worth being able to distinguish between them. The one you have just opened is labeled 'Command Prompt – essbase'.* ❜

Running `sample.exe`

Open another command prompt window (yes, we know things aren't improving yet) and navigate to the `c:\essbase\bin` directory. (*In fact, you may not need to move to the directory because it should now be included in the path. However, by moving there you ensure that you'll run the correct* `sample.exe` *if there happens to be more than one on your machine. We've known it to happen....*) Type `'sample'`.

A message tells you that running the `sample.exe` program will create the sample applications, and asks for the hostname.

Type it in and the DB2 OLAP Server supervisor ID – these are both the options you chose during installation. You will then be asked for the supervisor password which will, unnervingly, appear on screen as you type it. Make sure that no one is looking over your shoulder when you do so...

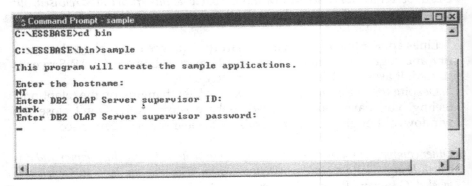

```
Command Prompt - sample                                    _ □ ×
C:\ESSBASE>cd bin

C:\ESSBASE\bin>sample

This program will create the sample applications.

Enter the hostname:
NT
Enter DB2 OLAP Server supervisor ID:
Mark
Enter DB2 OLAP Server supervisor password:
_
```

You'll see messages telling you that the sample applications are being created and that's it. Congratulations, you've created the sample applications. You can now close this window.

You should find that running sample.exe has created a number of extra command prompt windows that are open but minimised onto the Windows taskbar. You could ignore these: they don't all open up like this during a typical start of Essbase, only when you run sample.exe. However, to try to reduce the clutter we recommend that you now go to the one called 'Command Prompt – essbase' and type Quit. You will be asked if you are sure and when you answer in the affirmative, Essbase will close, taking all of the other command prompt windows with it. Once you have the C:\> command prompt back, simply type essbase again, enter the system password and Essbase will restart. From now on when you open an application, you'll get a single command prompt window for that application.

To inspect your progress, you should now introduce yourself to the Essbase Application Manager, and here, at last, we get back to GUIsville.

Starting the Application Manager

Navigate from the Start menu to IBM DB2 OLAP Server, Essbase Application Manager. And there it is, though it doesn't look too great yet.

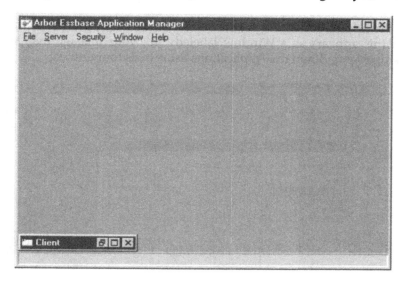

From the top menu, choose Server, Connect which opens the Essbase System Login dialog.

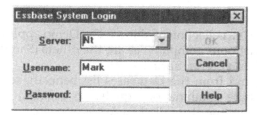

Check the Server and Username entries and enter the password (which **doesn't** appear on screen) – these again are the entries that you specified during installation. Click OK.

❻ *If you stop using the connection to Essbase for a period of more than 60 minutes (the default setting in Server, Settings, Inactive limit) it will decide that you've lost interest and will log you out automatically, but it won't shut down Essbase. This isn't a problem; if you start work again you will be asked if you want to re-connect and, once you have supplied the password, the connection will be re-made for you.*

As another aside, if you keep the 'Command Prompt – essbase' command prompt window open on screen, you'll see lines flitting past saying things like "Received client request: List Databases (from user Mark) etc.". There's no need to read them all, but the sight of activity in the window reassures you that something is happening.   ❾

In the Application Manager, the Server window appears. (In the screen shots this appears as a Window labeled 'Nt'; your mileage may vary). Clicking to pop down the Applications list reveals four entries.

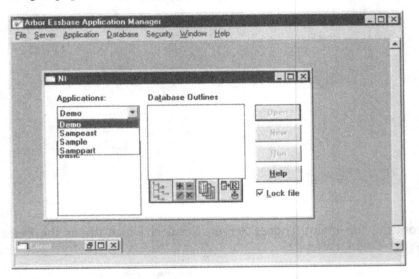

An application is a collection of objects. The Demo application is the data pertaining to a fictitious company, as are the others (Sample et al) and all were created when you ran `sample.exe`.

Select Demo, and from the Databases list beneath, select Basic. (Each application/database combination equates to a cube.) In the Database Outlines box, an outline also called Basic has appeared.

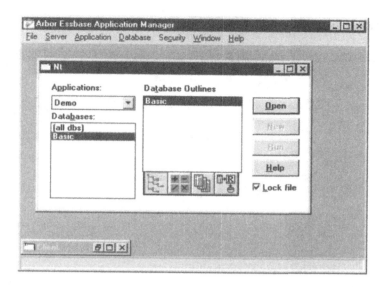

To recap briefly – the install program puts the files necessary to create the samples on the hard disk. Running `sample.exe` creates some sample data files. In addition, it also creates an empty cube structure. The one step it doesn't perform is the movement of data from those data files into that cube. In other words, the Demo application that you've chosen still doesn't contain any data. In OLAP parlance, the database has not yet been populated, or loaded, with data.

If you are keen, you can have a quick look at the data file that is going to be used for this process. The data file is called:

```
c:\essbase\app\demo\basic\data.txt
```

and it looks like this when viewed from Word:

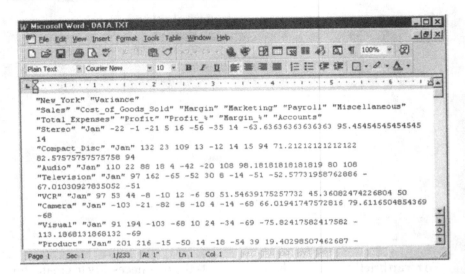

OK, so this may not be too informative, but we find it comforting at least to know what this sort of file looks like; we find that it helps to keep the process from becoming too abstract.

Once you've satisfied your curiosity, close Word. Then, to load the cube with data, from the top menu in the Essbase Application Manager, select Database, Load Data.

This Data Load dialog identifies the database (the one you've just chosen from those available). Click the Find button.

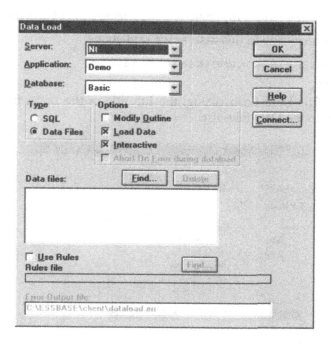

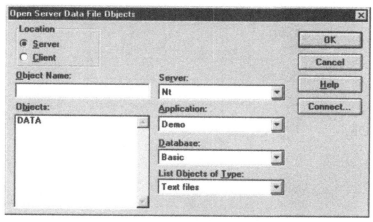

Click on DATA in the list of Objects (a very short list, this, containing nothing else) and your selection is transferred into the Object Name slot.

The selection in the List Objects of Type tells you that the DATA file is a text file. That text file is expected to be in the following location:

```
c:\essbase\app\appname\databasebname\filename.txt
```

or, more specifically in this case, as we said above:

```
c:\essbase\app\demo\basic\data.txt
```

Click on OK.

Back in the Data Load dialog, the full title of the DATA file has been entered into the Data Files list.

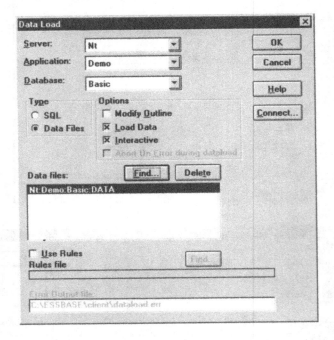

Click OK.

Messages appear saying 'Activating database' and 'Loading file', and then this dialog,

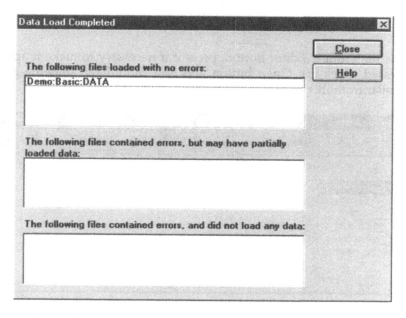

stating that the file was loaded with no errors.

Good; that's more progress. Once again, you may feel as if you're doing lots but achieving nothing. This is far from the case; despite the lack of apparent feedback you have created the sample applications and loaded data into the one called Demo. Let's take a closer look at the structure of the cube and the data.

Close the data loading dialog.

Outline Editor

In the Server window, which should still be open in the Application Manager, there are four colored buttons. If the dialog isn't open, look for the minimized title bar within the Application Manager window and open it up. (The dialog retreats into this mode if you close it as well as if you minimize it.)

The button on the far left shows a clutch of lines and boxes.

This is the Outline Editor button, press it if necessary to make it appear depressed. Click the Open button and you should see something not dissimilar from this.

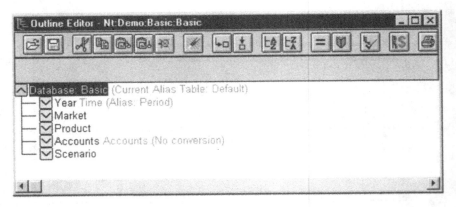

You are now looking at the Outline Editor. The Outline Editor is a great tool for showing the structure of the data in a cube. Data for use in OLAP cubes is highly hierarchical (sorry about the alliteration, see Chapter 13 for more details) and the Outline Editor provides a graphical representation of the hierarchy, called an outline. If you had built this cube by hand, you would have had to create this hierarchy, but here sample.exe has done it for you.

The top line identifies the database as Basic, which is what we expected. Beneath it and indented to the right are five dimensions. (Aha, **that** word re-emerges from the gloom).

To the left of each of the five dimensions and of the database is a small box showing an arrow. Double click the up arrow alongside Basic. The five dimensions beneath it vanish, and the arrow now points downwards.

Double click it again. You will no doubt have gathered that, as with many outlining tools, you can roll up and roll down the layers of detail to obtain exactly the view you want. When no arrow is visible in the box, there are no further layers to unroll.

There is a lot in this Basic example, as you can see if you start unrolling the layers. Items, such as Qtr1 and Profit, that appear beneath each dimension, are the members.

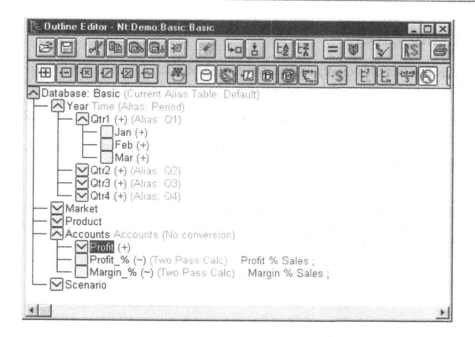

With all the layers visible, you wouldn't be able to see everything at once and would have to scroll up and down.

OK, so that's the hierarchy to which the data conforms, but we seem to be no nearer looking at the actual data. Fear not, that comes next.

Viewing data

The Essbase Application Manager does not provide a tool for looking at the actual values in a cube. That functionality is typically provided by an additional tool. Many people choose to use a specialized tool, such as those provided by Cognos, Business Objects and Brio. *In fact, DB2 OLAP Server is available bundled with specialized data manipulation tools (see Appendix 2).*

Other people use a spreadsheet as that tool; anyone who has used pivot tables in Excel or the equivalent in Lotus 1-2-3 will already be familiar with the spreadsheet take on multiple dimensions. You'll probably be happy to learn that add-ins for using IBM's own Lotus 1-2-3 and Microsoft Excel are ready and waiting.

Using Excel

This demo could equally well be done with Lotus 1-2-3. *The fact that we chose Excel isn't a recommendation, we just think that, since Microsoft's Office is the best selling suite of programs out there, Excel is the application that you are most likely to have immediately available.* Start Excel, open a blank spreadsheet and click on Tools, Add-Ins....

Click the Browse button and navigate to c:\essbase\bin where you should find a file called

    essexcln.xll

This is the Essbase Excel client software. Highlight it and click OK.

If you look through the selected add-ins, you should find that Arbor Essbase OLAP Server DLL is checked,

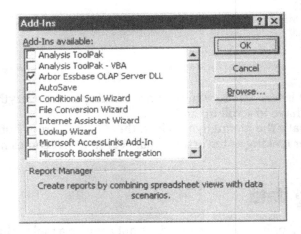

so click OK.

The Arbor splash screen appears briefly, and on inspecting the Excel menu you'll see that a new item, Essbase, has been added.

From this Essbase menu, click Connect and type the password in the login dialog. Press Enter and a list of the available application/database combinations appears below. These are the samples you've already seen listed in the Essbase Application Manager.

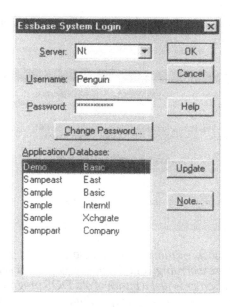

Highlight Demo/Basic and click OK. The dialog vanishes and you're left looking at a blank Excel worksheet. From the Essbase menu, select Retrieve. Labels and a single value appears on the sheet.

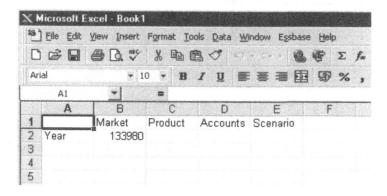

Bingo: data! At last!

❻ *You may remember that earlier we said that you would be opening another command prompt window. The action you have just taken, making a connection to the cube, has just opened this second window. You may well not have noticed because it will be sitting quietly on the taskbar. However, you can open it up if you wish, just to have a look. It will be called 'Essbase Server – Demo'. It is good idea not to tease it at this stage (say, by closing it down): we only mention it so that you know what is going on.*

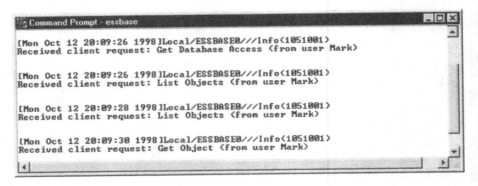

Once you've had a look, minimize it (don't close it!) and get back to Excel.

Just in case you were worrying, all this command prompt activity does not indicate that DB2 OLAP Server is just a bunch of old DOS programs. Each application runs its own process in a command prompt window, and each is a fully-blown 32-bit NT process. ❾

To expand a dimension or member, you double click on it. So double click Market and you should see this

	A	B	C	D	E
1			Product	Accounts	Scenario
2	East	Year	46576		
3	West	Year	62839		
4	South	Year	24565		
5	Market	Year	133980		
6					

and then do the same for the Year cell alongside East, to show the figures per quarter.

	A	B	C	D	E
1			Product	Accounts	Scenario
2	East	Qtr1	10420		
3		Qtr2	7276		
4		Qtr3	11280		
5		Qtr4	17600		
6		Year	46576		
7	West	Qtr1	12917		
8		Qtr2	11449		
9		Qtr3	14270		
10		Qtr4	24203		
11		Year	62839		
12	South	Qtr1	4474		
13		Qtr2	4199		
14		Qtr3	5430		
15		Qtr4	10462		
16		Year	24565		
17	Market	Qtr1	27811		
18		Qtr2	22924		
19		Qtr3	30980		
20		Qtr4	52265		
21		Year	133980		
22					

It's easy to move dimensions around too. On the cell labeled Product, click and hold down the right mouse button. A floating label appears which says 'Product Accounts Scenario'. Drag this label over to cell A2; the floating label now reads 'Product'. Release the mouse button.

	A	B	C	D	E
1				Accounts	Scenario
2	Product	East	Qtr1	10420	
3			Qtr2	7276	
4			Qtr3	11280	
5			Qtr4	17600	
6			Year	46576	
7		West	Qtr1	12917	
8			Qtr2	11449	
9			Qtr3	14270	
10			Qtr4	24203	
11			Year	62839	
12		South	Qtr1	4474	
13			Qtr2	4199	
14			Qtr3	5430	
15			Qtr4	10462	
16			Year	24565	
17		Market	Qtr1	27811	
18			Qtr2	22924	
19			Qtr3	30980	
20			Qtr4	52265	
21			Year	133980	
22					

The Product dimension is now in the first column, and double clicking it expands it to show sales per quarter for each product line.

	A	B	C	D	E
1				Accounts	Scenario
2	Audio	East	Qtr1	3077	
3			Qtr2	2532	
4			Qtr3	2976	
5			Qtr4	4853	
6			Year	13438	
7		West	Qtr1	4875	
8			Qtr2	4320	
9			Qtr3	5324	
10			Qtr4	7969	
11			Year	22488	
12		South	Qtr1	0	
13			Qtr2	0	
14			Qtr3	0	
15			Qtr4	0	
16			Year	0	
17		Market	Qtr1	7952	
18			Qtr2	6852	
19			Qtr3	8300	
20			Qtr4	12822	
21			Year	35926	
22	Visual	East	Qtr1	7343	
23			Qtr2	4744	
24			Qtr3	8304	
25			Qtr4	12747	

To collapse a level, double click with the right mouse button. For example, to undo your last action, double right click on the Audio label in cell A2.

Playtime

Now is the time to have a serious play with this view of the data from within Excel. Experiment with expanding and collapsing levels, and with moving dimensions between the axes, whatever takes your fancy. You've done some work to get here, now is the time to have fun. It is a good idea to keep flipping back to the Application Manager and relating what you can see of the cube structure with the data that you can see in Excel.

Help

There's a good help system for using the Excel add-in that's reached from the Start menu via Programs, IBM DB2 OLAP Server, Essbase Excel Add-In Help. There is a great deal of functionality in the add-in, as will quickly become apparent if you wander through the help for a spell. We don't have the space here to cover much beyond the very basics of looking at data, but if you're an Excel user you should find things to your liking. The same type of help is available for Lotus 1-2-3, so you are covered either way.

Recap

Following the creation of the sample applications, you have populated a cube with data. You have inspected the hierarchical structure of the Demo:Basic cube using the Essbase Application Manager. You have also inspected (and briefly manipulated) the actual values available within the cube from Excel via the excellent Essbase Excel/Lotus 1-2-3 add-in.

Just to make the story complete, you didn't have to build the hierarchical structure, nor did you have to create the data file. In addition, the data file provided by `sample.exe` was unusual in that it provided all of the data for all of the members. This means that you didn't have to calculate the data for the higher level members. This isn't a problem; we just point it out here in case you were waiting for that step somewhere. (If you were it means that you have an excellent grasp of what's going on. Award yourself a gold star. If you hadn't noticed, don't worry; there is a lot to take in here, which is precisely why `sample.exe` does so much for you).

And remember, you are the data warehouse administrator, sitting at one NT machine making a connection from Excel to the data in the cube. However, once you make an operational cube, your users will also be able to connect into the cube from Excel or 1-2-3 in essentially the same way, across the network.

In Chapter 16 we'll have more of a look at the Application Manager and then in Chapter 17 we'll show you how to create your own cube structure from scratch and populate it with data. However, before we do that, we'll show you how to shut down everything that is running at the moment. You don't have to do this now, you could go straight on to Chapter 16, but going by our experience, we always like to know how to back out elegantly from applications. In addition, you may well feel that you have learnt enough for today. Have a break after you have closed everything down; go on, you've earned your reward of a hot chocolate/stiff martini/whatever.

Closing everything down

Closing Excel

When you've finished, click Disconnect in the Essbase menu. In the Disconnect dialog, click the Disconnect button and then on Close. The worksheet remains visible, but the data in Essbase is no longer available. Double clicking on a member brings up the Essbase System Login dialog to enable you to reconnect should you wish. The act of closing down Excel will also disconnect it from Essbase.

Closing the Application Manager

Simply closing the Application Manager disconnects it from Essbase. Should you wish to disconnect manually, click Server, Disconnect, and the OK button in the Logout dialog. Use the exit button or File, Exit to close Application Manager itself.

Closing Essbase

Pull up the window called 'Command Prompt – essbase'. It will tell you that you have logged out (this happened when you closed the Application Manager) but Essbase itself is still running.

Type 'quit' (or 'exit') to stop Essbase. You'll be asked if you want to 'Stop all applications and exit Essbase?'. Type 'y' and eventually you'll see the message below, confirming that all activity has ceased.

```
Command Prompt                                              _ □ ×
quit

Executing command: QUIT

Stop all applications and exit Essbase [y/n]?y
[Wed Sep 30 14:07:25 1998]Local/ESSBASE0///Info(1054005)
Shutting down application Demo

[Wed Sep 30 14:07:33 1998]Local/ESSBASE0///Info(1051052)
Arbor Essbase OLAP Server - finished

C:\>
```

In the meantime, very quietly, and without any fuss, the other command prompt window called 'Essbase Server – Demo' will have been shut down for you. Good. Essbase has now been shut down and you can manually close the window called 'Command Prompt – essbase' by typing 'exit' at the prompt.

Chapter 16

More about the Outline Editor

Where you are

If Essbase isn't running, fire it up, open up the Application Manager, connect to Essbase and open the Demo:Basic database outline. You are allowed to refer to Chapter 15, but you get extra points if you can do all of this from memory.

This chapter is short and simply goes into slightly more detail about the Application Manager.

More about the Outline Editor

The Outline Editor shows a hierarchical view of the dimensions and members that define the structure of the cube. We've already covered some of the concepts and terminology that you need; here's where you see them in action and meet a few more.

Dimensions

The dimensions in the Demo:Basic cube are Year, Market, Product, Accounts and Scenario.

Members

Dimensions have members. Thus Qtr1 is a member of the dimension Year, as is Jan.

Dimension types

The buttons that appear at the top of the window change as you highlight different dimensions. Dimensions can be (but certainly don't **have** to be) of different predefined types. For example, Year is of type Time, Accounts is of type Accounts. You can set the type for a dimension using these buttons.

We said that you don't have to use these predefined types, but it helps if you use them when appropriate. Why? Because it enables DB2 OLAP Server to provide you with built-in features for data of that type. For example, if you highlight Accounts (which is of type Accounts) you discover that extra accounting-type buttons appear on the button bar.

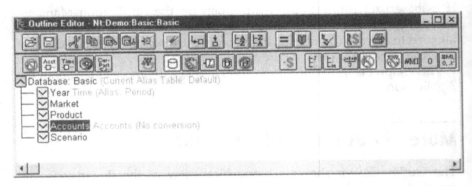

Hierarchy descriptions

The hierarchic structure displayed by the Outline Editor can be described in two ways, either by reading down the branches from the top down to the bottom, or by reading up the branches from the bottom to the top.

Generation

Working from top to bottom, the steps are counted in generations starting at generation 1. Thus Year, Market, Product etc. are generation 1. Expanding these shows Qtr1, East etc. which are generation 2 and so on.

There is no need for the tree to be entirely 'symmetrical'. By that we mean that all branches don't have to have the same number of generations.

As the screen shot shows, Jan is a bottom level generation and is generation number 3, whereas Actual is also at the bottom, but is only generation 2.

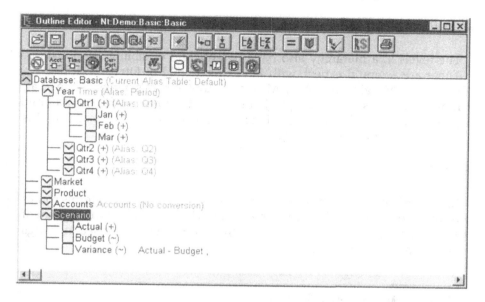

Level

You can also work from the bottom to the top. This approach works in levels, with Level 0 (no, not Level 1 as you might have expected) being the lowest level.

Any level which cannot be further expanded is counted as level 0. Thus Actual is at level 0, as is Jan. This means that Scenario is at level 1, as is East.

Now, before you work it out for yourself, we'll point out that this appears to introduce an anomaly. Take the two dimensions Year and Scenario.

Mar is at level 0, so Qtr1 must be level 1 and Year must be level 2 – fine so far.

Actual is level 0, so Scenario is level 1 – no problem.

So Year (level 2) and Scenario (level 1) are at different levels, but if we count from the top down we find that they belong to the same generation – namely 1.

Can this be right? Yes, it's fine. These 'naming systems' are there for your convenience, nothing more. At any one time it may be convenient to say "If we go up a level to level 3...". At another time it may be easier to say "moving down to generation 2...". We worried about the 'anomaly' when we first met it, but it doesn't cause any problems in practice and so it isn't really anomalous.

Child/sibling/parent

The levels in a hierarchy also have parent/child or sibling relationships. These are as you'd expect, with Jan being a child of Qtr1, Profit being a parent of Margin, and Apr, May and June being siblings. Note that, however, Apr isn't a sibling of Jan because they have different parents. (Note also that children have only one parent, but that's OK as well in this modern, non-nuclear, society).

Leaf

Level 0 members can also be called leaves or leaf nodes – these terms comes from the tree view of the outline hierarchy. The root is the starting point of any branch, i.e. the dimension. No further woody terms are used, no twigs or boughs – shame really.

Consolidation objects

The outline view shows mathematical operators after each member; these are known as consolidation objects. These indicate how the members interact to produce the data in the member (or dimension) in the next level up.

Look at the outline view below.

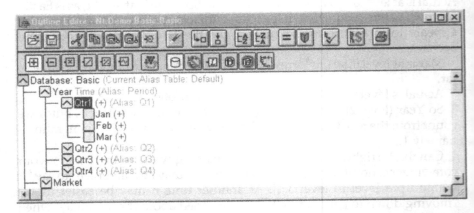

❻ *The consolidation objects are blue in the outline, a fact sadly lost in the screenshots.* ❾

The plus symbol alongside the members Jan, Feb and March shows that these three values are added together to give the value in Qrt1. The plus symbols alongside the members Qtr1, Qtr2, Qtr3 and Qtr4 indicate that the values in each of these are added to produce the value in Year.

If we look at the expanded Accounts dimension,

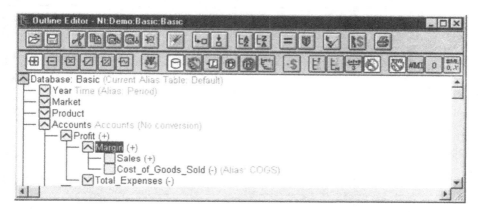

we see that the value in Margin is arrived at by subtracting the value in Cost_of_Goods_Sold from Sales, and that the value in Profit comes from subtracting Total_Expenses from Margin.

Each member has a consolidation object; the default is +. Other consolidation objects are +, –, *, / and %, and members can be excluded from any consolidation with the ~ symbol.

The Outline Editor defaults to showing consolidation objects, but you can turn them off by selecting View from the Application Manager menu and unchecking the Consolidation Objects option.

The six consolidation objects buttons to the left of the lower button set the consolidation object for the highlighted member.

Formula objects

The examples of consolidation given above use values from members in the same generation, but it is also possible to derive values from members in different generations. To do this a two pass calculation must be specified, to ensure that up-to-date values are available.

Look to the right of the Profit_% member: it says, in green and in brackets, Two Pass Calc, and to the right of that, Profit % Sales.

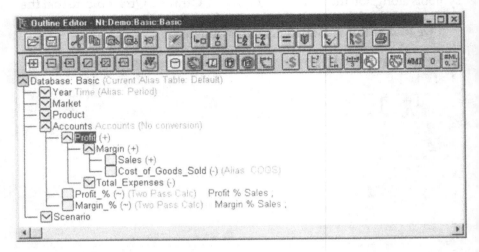

If you inspect the hierarchy of the Accounts dimension, you'll see that the two values used to calculate Profit_%, namely Profit and Sales, are Generation 2 and Generation 4 respectively.

Values are generated using the consolidation objects described above, and in a second pass, the consolidated values can be used to calculate further values.

Formula objects can also be rendered invisible by selecting Formula Objects from View in the Application Manager menu.

The button to the right of the consolidation object buttons inserts a two pass calculation formula object.

You can inspect the formula for Profit_% by highlighting it and clicking the button in the top row which carries an 'equals' sign.

which opens this dialog.

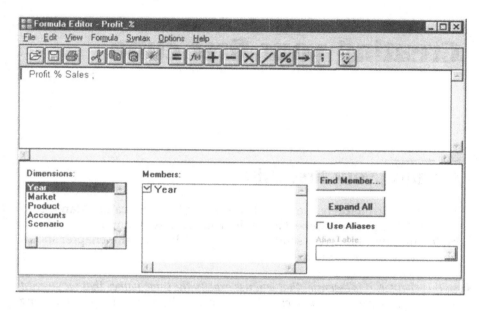

You can also use this dialog to generate new formula for other members, but we suggest that you don't do this in the sample file unless you are really sure you know what you are doing.

What's next?

Next we'll put all this into practice and build a cube from scratch. Chapter 17 is where it all happens.

Creating your first cube

Creating your first cube

In the last two chapters, we've looked at using the Application Manager to manipulate a pre-built cube. Hopefully you are now champing at the bit to build your own cube from scratch. That's good, because this chapter shows you how to do precisely that.

❦ *In this chapter, it is essential that you use exactly the same names that we suggest for the dimensions, members etc. If you accidentally misspell one (say, using Hering instead of Herring), then the data load will fail. However, if you **do** happen to make such a mistake, don't worry, we show you how to correct it.* ❧

Creating an application

Assuming that you are starting afresh, fire up Essbase and open the Application Manager. Connect to the server and the Server window should open. Click on File, New, Application. Give the application a name (this one is called Fish) and check that the Server option is selected as the Location in order to create the new application on the server.

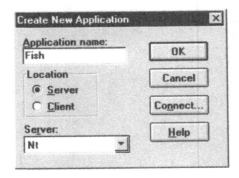

Click OK. You are returned to the Application Manager, and in the
Server window, Fish is now listed as an available application.

Creating a database

The next step is to create a database within that application, so click File,
New, Database. Give it a name: we use Basic.

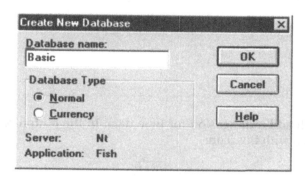

❝ *'Basic' is the traditional name for the first database in an OLAP application, rather
in the way that "Hello World" is every programmer's first program. Of course,
many programmers wrote their "Hello World" program in BASIC, but let's not get
too recursive...* ❞

Leave the Database Type as Normal; the Currency option is for databases that will need to convert between different currencies. Click OK

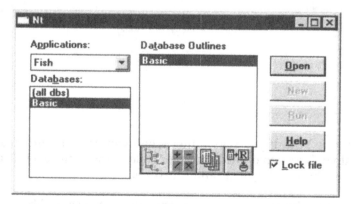

and there it is in the Database list for the new Fish application. Check the
Outline Editor button is depressed and click Open.

Creating an outline

The Outline Editor opens with a single highlighted entry, that for the Basic database.

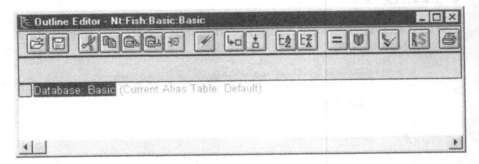

First we'll add a dimension for time data. In the button bar is an Add Child button with this icon:

Put the cursor over it and in the bottom left of the screen, you'll see a description of its action. Click the button. A child member appears with a box and blinking cursor, ready to receive a name.

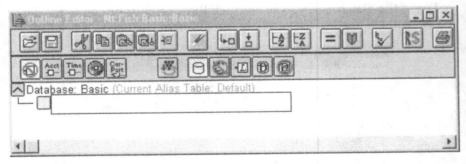

Call this one Year. If you press Enter when you finish typing Year, you'll find that you've elected to add another child at the same level. That's fine; add dimensions for Products and Measures.

❧ *Measures is another traditional term for accounting information, like profits, costs, margins and so on.* ❧

To stop adding members at this level, after typing the final s in Measures, click the cursor elsewhere in the hierarchy to remove the focus from the addition process. If you accidentally press the Enter key and start the process of creating a new dimension, simply press Esc. (That last sentence sounds too much like science fiction to be true, but it isn't.)

If you have made a mistake in any of these names, simply right click on the name and correct it.

Now add some child members to Year. Highlight Year, click the Add Child button and add four child members for quarterly figures called Q1, Q2, Q3 and Q4. Add four child members for products under Products called Herring, Salmon, Plaice and Trout. Add a child member to Measures called Profit, and add two child members called Sales and Costs to Profit.

❝*A dimension, by the way, can contain an effectively unlimited number of members, reaching the hundreds of thousands.* ❞

Your outline should look like this.

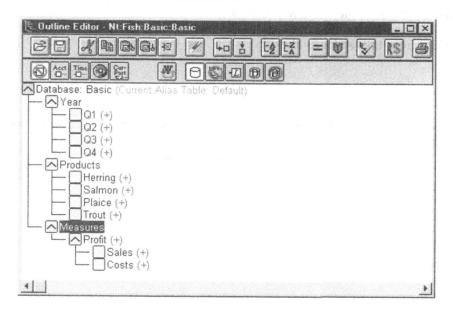

Adding consolidation objects

Check out the symbols alongside the members; they all show the default of +. That's fine for everything except for the Costs member, where Costs should have a subtraction symbol (–).

Highlight Costs, and look at the second row of buttons. The second from the left shows a subtraction sign; click it. The consolidation object for Costs is changed from + to –.

Adding dimension types

The Application Manager has four ready-made dimension types, Time, Accounts, Country and Currency. Defining a dimension as a specific type allows it to access built-in functions designed for that type.

We won't be making use of these functions in this example, but we'll designate a couple to show you how.

Click on Year in the outline and look at the second row of buttons. The third from the left looks like this:

and clicking it adds the dimension type Time (in red) after the Year dimension.

Highlight Measures and click the Account dimension type button:

and your outline should now look like this.

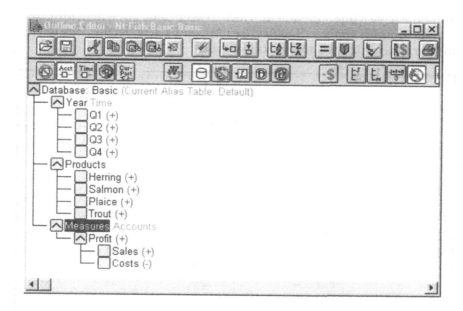

Saving an outline

Simply click the Save button.

Messages flit past about activating and then restructuring the database, and that's it.

Adding data

You now have a fine structure in which to keep data, but where's the data to come from? It's on the CD-ROM (see Appendix 3 for details). The data in the file is tab separated and looks like this:

Year	Products	Measures	
Q1	Herring	Sales	23
Q1	Salmon	Sales	14
Q1	Plaice	Sales	4
Q1	Trout	Sales	17
Q1	Herring	Costs	13
Q1	Salmon	Costs	7
Q1	Plaice	Costs	1
Q1	Trout	Costs	9
Q2	Herring	Sales	12
Q2	Salmon	Sales	9
Q2	Plaice	Sales	34
Q2	Trout	Sales	20
Q2	Herring	Costs	5
Q2	Salmon	Costs	3
Q2	Plaice	Costs	25
Q2	Trout	Costs	8
Q3	Herring	Sales	14

We say 'like this' because this only shows the header row and the first 17 rows of data while the actual file has 32 rows of data. However, these simply continue the good work and provide data for all four quarters. By all means have a look at the file itself using your favorite text editor. Then copy the text file to the Basic database directory

```
c:\essbase\app\fish\basic\fish.txt
```

❦ *The files from read-only CD-ROMS usually remain read-only when copied; if you want to do anything other than read them, you'll have to use your NT skills to remove this restriction. Hint, from Explorer, right click the file...* ❦

Close the Outline Editor, and from the Application Manager menu, click Database, Load Data...

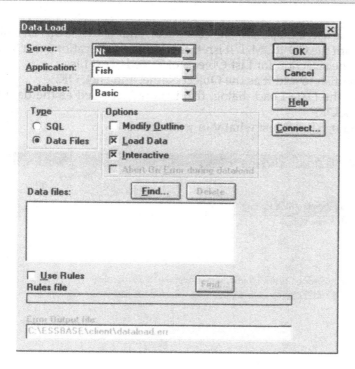

The Fish:Basic application and database combination are already in place,
and the data load Type is set to Data Files. The Load Data and Interactive
options are set, but as yet there are no files listed under Data files.
   Click the Find... button.

There in the list of Objects is one called fish – this is the `fish.txt` file you copied from the CD-ROM. If it isn't, check that the Location is set to Server and that the selection for List Objects of Type is Text files.

Click on fish to add it as the Object Name, and click OK.

Back in the Data Load dialog, fish is now identified as the data file to load. Click OK.

This dialog shows just what you want to see.

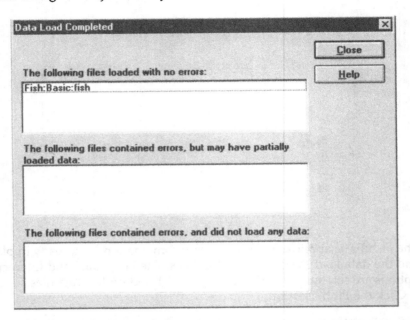

Click Close and all should be well. If the data load fails, read the error message that appears. The most likely cause is a misspelt name, so go back to the outline, make the necessary change and try again.

Recap

Thus far you have created an application and a database within it, and you've determined the structure the data will have. You've also loaded in the data from a text (flat) file which will have put data in place at the leaf nodes; in other words, only Level 0 data exists in the Basic database.

This is perfectly logical when you consider the contents of the original data. It contained no calculated fields at all; there were no totals for the number of salmon sold in a year, no profits calculated by subtracting costs from sales.

The data from the text file was put into the lowest level of the database outline, and all the calculating and summarizing remains to be done, and we'll do it next.

❛ *If you wish to see the current situation for yourself, start Excel with the Essbase add-in (details in Chapter 14) and retrieve Fish:Basic. Your raw sales and costs data is present, but all the other fields say '#Missing'.* ❜

	A	B	C	D	E	F
1			Sales	Costs	Profit	Measures
2	Herring	Q1	23	13	#Missing	#Missing
3		Q2	12	5	#Missing	#Missing
4		Q3	14	5	#Missing	#Missing
5		Q4	45	15	#Missing	#Missing
6		Year	#Missing	#Missing	#Missing	#Missing
7	Salmon	Q1	14	7	#Missing	#Missing
8		Q2	9	3	#Missing	#Missing
9		Q3	3	2	#Missing	#Missing
10		Q4	9	4	#Missing	#Missing
11		Year	#Missing	#Missing	#Missing	#Missing
12	Plaice	Q1	4	1	#Missing	#Missing
13		Q2	34	25	#Missing	#Missing
14		Q3	11	5	#Missing	#Missing
15		Q4	23	14	#Missing	#Missing
16		Year	#Missing	#Missing	#Missing	#Missing
17	Trout	Q1	17	9	#Missing	#Missing
18		Q2	20	8	#Missing	#Missing
19		Q3	24	12	#Missing	#Missing
20		Q4	17	9	#Missing	#Missing
21		Year	#Missing	#Missing	#Missing	#Missing
22	Products	Q1	#Missing	#Missing	#Missing	#Missing
23		Q2	#Missing	#Missing	#Missing	#Missing
24		Q3	#Missing	#Missing	#Missing	#Missing
25		Q4	#Missing	#Missing	#Missing	#Missing
26		Year	#Missing	#Missing	#Missing	#Missing
27						

❛ *You may wonder why the calculation step was not performed when we looked at the sample application, Demo. It was because the data files provided by* `sample.exe` *supply data for all levels, not just level 0.* ❜

Calculating data

From the Application Manager menu, select Database, Calculate...

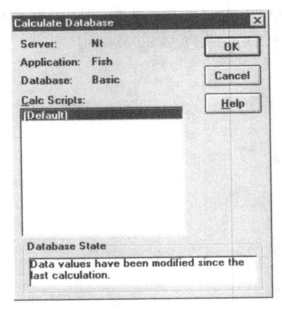

Just click the OK button in the Calculate Database dialog, you'll see a message that calculation is occurring, and then everything returns to normal. This absence of information is a good sign; the calculation is complete and the data in the Basic database is now complete.

Checking the data is present

We'll use Excel again to view the data we've just loaded, so fire up that worthy spreadsheet and activate the Essbase add-in if this isn't already done (see Chapter 14 for how to do this) and connect to Essbase.

From the list of applications and databases, highlight the Fish:Basic combination and click OK. Click Essbase, Retrieve.

	A	B	C
1		Products	Measures
2	Year		142
3			
4			

Well, that's not a lot to show for all your hard work, is it? Double click on Year, however, and you'll see that everything is fine. You can expand the levels and move the dimensions to show whatever fishy view you wish.

	A	B	C Sales	D Costs	E Profit	F Measures
1						
2	Herring	Q1	23	13	10	10
3		Q2	12	5	7	7
4		Q3	14	5	9	9
5		Q4	45	15	30	30
6		Year	94	38	56	56
7	Salmon	Q1	14	7	7	7
8		Q2	9	3	6	6
9		Q3	3	2	1	1
10		Q4	9	4	5	5
11		Year	35	16	19	19
12	Plaice	Q1	4	1	3	3
13		Q2	34	25	9	9
14		Q3	11	5	6	6
15		Q4	23	14	9	9
16		Year	72	45	27	27
17	Trout	Q1	17	9	8	8
18		Q2	20	8	12	12
19		Q3	24	12	12	12
20		Q4	17	9	8	8
21		Year	78	38	40	40
22	Products	Q1	58	30	28	28
23		Q2	75	41	34	34
24		Q3	52	24	28	28
25		Q4	94	42	52	52
26		Year	279	137	142	142
27						

6 *You'll notice that the values in Measures and Profit are identical at present. That's because our example has room for expansion and improvement. For instance, Profit could acquire a sibling called Total_Expenses and the data therein could be used to divulge further information.* 9

DB2 tables

Let's have a quick look at DB2's take on all this. This step isn't necessary, but as always it's interesting to see what goes on behind the scenes.

❢ *We'll look at the actual tables here, but we're not suggesting you'd do this operationally; instead, you'd use the Views that DB2 OLAP Server creates and manages.* ❡

In the Control Center, inspect the list of tables in the DB2OLAP database. Look for a table called CUBECATALOG and inspect its sample contents.

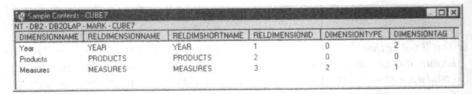

APPNAME	CUBENAME	RELAPPNAME	RELCUBENAME	RELCUBEID	RELCUE
Demo	Basic	DEMO	BASI	1	100
Sample	Basic	SAMP	BASI	2	100
Sample	Interntl	SAMP	INTE	3	100
Sample	Xchgrate	SAMP	XCHG	4	100
Sampeast	East	SAM1	EAST	5	100
Samppart	Company	SAM2	COMP	6	100
Fish	Basic	FISH	BASI	7	100

Sample Contents - CUBECATALOG — NT - DB2 - DB2OLAP - MARK - CUBECATALOG

Each entry is for an application/database combination (i.e. a cube) and in the column RELCUBEID is a number that identifies each uniquely. In our case, Fish/Basic is number 7 (it may not be the same for you). Return to the list of tables and scroll down to a table called CUBE7 and look at its contents.

DIMENSIONNAME	RELDIMENSIONNAME	RELDIMSHORTNAME	RELDIMENSIONID	DIMENSIONTYPE	DIMENSIONTAG
Year	YEAR	YEAR	1	0	2
Products	PRODUCTS	PRODUCTS	2	0	0
Measures	MEASURES	MEASURES	3	2	1

Sample Contents - CUBE7 — NT - DB2 - DB2OLAP - MARK - CUBE7

Here are the three dimensions used in the cube, with various pieces of information for the unhesitating identification of each by the software. Year is dimension 1, Products is 2 and so on. Take a look at a few more tables; CUBE7DIM2 contains the members of the Products dimension, for instance. There is an enormous weight of tables behind each cube; your users don't have to look at them, even you don't have to, but it is worth knowing that behind every cube is a set of tables that can and should be backed up, just like a normal DB2 database.

Sparse and dense dimensions

You'll remember we mentioned these in Chapter 13, but in the above example they're ignored. In the background, quietly and automatically, the software has identified each dimension as sparse or dense. In a tiny database like this, it is perfectly safe and indeed sensible to leave the choice of sparse and dense dimensions to Essbase.

It is, however, true that an understanding of sparse and dense dimensions will let you build applications which can be stored more efficiently and from which data can be retrieved more rapidly. While Essbase can decide automatically which of the dimensions in your outline are sparse and which are dense, it can only make an educated guess because it cannot tell what data you'll be loading.

When identifying sparse dimensions, it is noticeable that these usually occur in multiples. In the example used earlier (people making sales at the store where they're employed and nowhere else), there are two sparse dimensions, People and Store. Similarly, if a business decision was made to sell a subset of products in some stores, the dimensions storing products and geographical data would both be sparse.

Inspecting and defining sparse/dense dimensions

To check the current selections, or to re-define them yourself, use the Outline Editor to open an outline. Here we'll look at the Demo:Basic outline (as opposed to the Fish:Basic one that we've used up until now in this chapter). Click Settings, Data Storage... in the main menu. The Data Storage dialog opens; click the Recommend button.

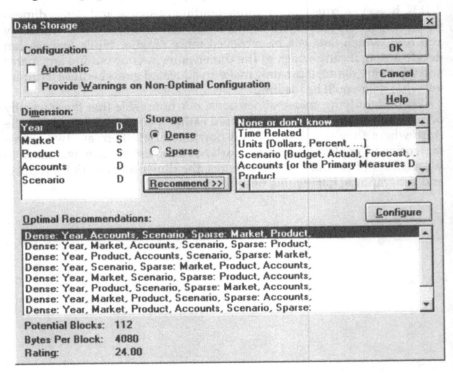

The choices that have been made fit the foregoing broad generalizations above. Product and Market are sparse dimensions, and Year, Measures and Scenario are dense. (Measures, like Time, is a classically dense dimension).

If you know your data well enough to gainsay any of the choices made automatically, you can make changes in this dialog.

Recap

Well, that's it – you've produced your first cube of data. It's small, it's simple but it's perfectly formed and you're already started on the path to greater things. You've calculated all the data above the leaf nodes in the database hierarchy, inspected the results and played with expanding levels and moving dimensions around.

There are things you can do to improve the performance of a cube, and one of the most important of these is to choose a suitable anchor dimension. This new term is explained in Chapter 19, and we also give guidelines for choosing the best one.

Chapter 18

Data load rules

Rules files

You can, as we did in the last chapter, load the entire contents of a suitably formatted data file, but you can also choose to load in a subset of data, or data from a source in a less suitable format. This is done using a Rules file. The data is loaded just as before, but a Rules file is associated with the process, and it is this file that determines exactly what data is transferred.

There is a text file called `addfish.txt` (also on the CD-ROM – see Appendix 3) which contains costs and sales records for halibut and cod. It looks like this:

Q1	Halibut	Sales	6
Q1	Cod	Sales	8
Q1	Halibut	Costs	4
Q1	Cod	Costs	4
Q2	Halibut	Sales	10
Q2	Cod	Sales	12
Q2	Halibut	Costs	5

(As before, this isn't the complete set, just enough to give you the idea).

Copy this file to `c:\essbase\app\fish\basic`.

From this, we want to add only the halibut data into the Fish:Basic database, ignoring the cod records.

In order to add halibut records there has to be somewhere to put them, so we need to add a new member to the outline.

Editing the outline

Open the Outline Editor and expand the Products dimension. Highlight Products, click the Add Child button and name it Halibut (*"I name this child 'Halibut'"* – *surely nobody could be so mean*).

The Halibut member is placed at the top of the list, but if you want to move it to below Trout, click and drag Halibut on top of Trout and release. Make sure you don't drag too far over to the right or Halibut will become a child of Trout instead of a sibling.

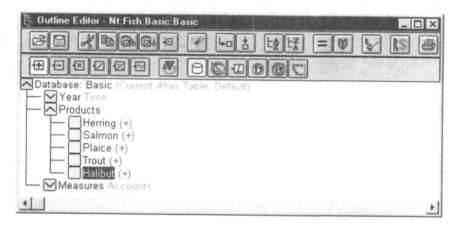

Save the new outline by clicking on the Save button (the second button on the top button bar). The Restructure Database dialog opens.

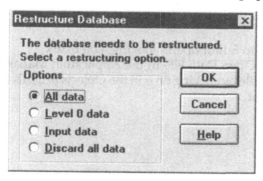

Leave the All data option selected and click OK. Close the Outline Editor. Now you can start work on the Rules file.

Building a rules file

In the Application Manager, click on the last button on the right, the one with this icon:

This is the Data Load Rules button. (*"Data Load Rules OK", as one of our proof-readers said.*) You'll see there are no rules at present. Click New

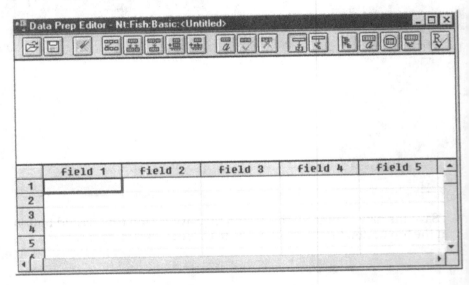

and the Data Prep Editor opens, looking a bit blank.

Click on File, Open Data File in the Application Manager menu. Select the addfish text file by clicking on it in the Objects list; this inserts it into the Object Name slot.

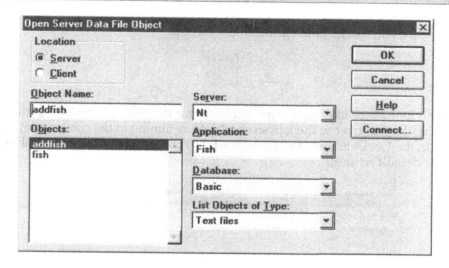

Click OK.

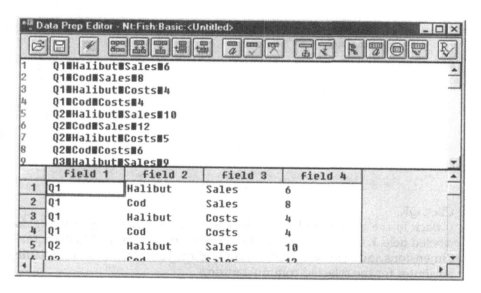

This is what you should see; the raw data source is in the top part of the window and the grid in the lower part shows the appearance of the data after the rule has been applied. As you can see, both halibut and cod records are visible.

247

Click the 'Set the data file attributes' button:

(this looks very like the 'Define attributes for the selected column' button that's further over to the left, so check you're aiming at the correct one).

In the File Delimiter tab, check that Tab is chosen as the delimiter (Tab is the default setting).

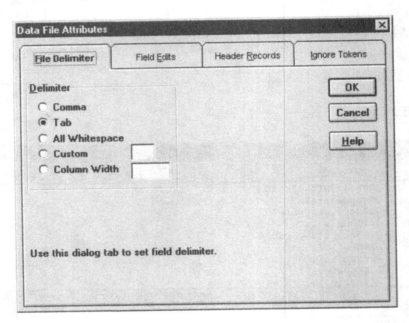

Click OK.

Back in the Data Prep Editor window, at the top of the grid are fields labeled field 1, field 2 and so on. These fields must be mapped to the actual dimensions and members used in your outline. To do this, click the 'Define attributes for the selected column' button.

Select the Data Load Attributes tab.

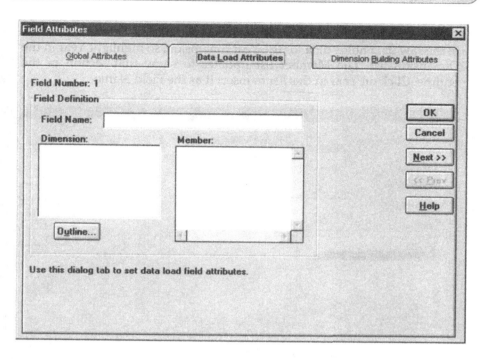

There are no dimensions or members listed because this new Rule is not yet associated with any outline file. Click the Outline... button and navigate to the Basic outline, clicking on it in the Objects list to insert it as the Object Name. Click OK.

Now the dimensions and members from your outline are shown. Field 1 in the raw data holds data for the Year dimension, so highlight Year in the Dimension list. The Member list updates to show that section of the outline. Click on Year in this list to insert it as the Field Name.

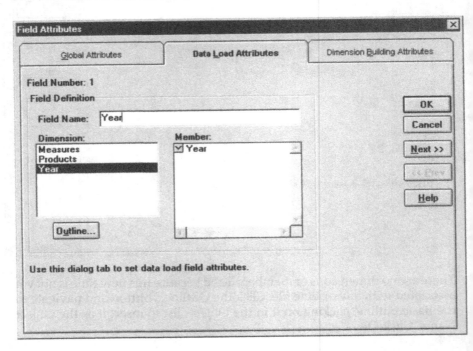

Now click the Next button and select Products as the field name for field 2, and repeat the process for the Measures field (field 3). Click Next.

The fourth field is slightly different, holding references to members, rather than to a dimension. It contains entries for two members: these are Sales and Costs from the Measures dimension. With Measures highlighted in the Dimensions list, expand the outline in the Members list till you can see Sales and Costs. Click Sales, type a comma from the keyboard and click Costs.

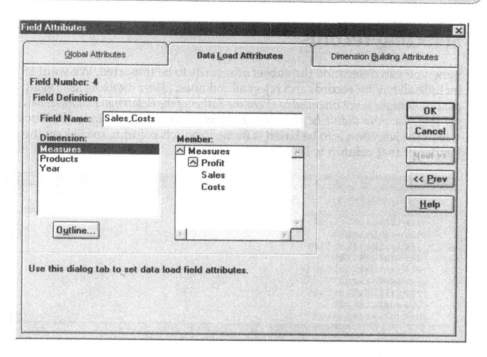

All four fields now have names, so click OK. The new names appear at the top of the grid, as you can see in the next screen shot.

Selecting records

Now you can determine the subset of records to be imported. We want to include all halibut records and reject all cod ones. (*There's nothing fishy going on; this example is not intended to slight the Father of the Relational Database, he's got two 'd's. And didn't he also coin the term 'OLAP'?*) The information on which the selection is to be based is in the Products column, so click on the header of that column to highlight it.

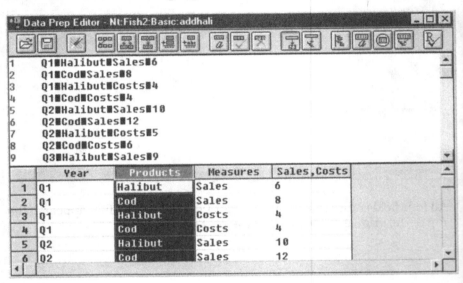

Then click on the 'Set record selection criteria for the selected column' button

to open the Select Record dialog.

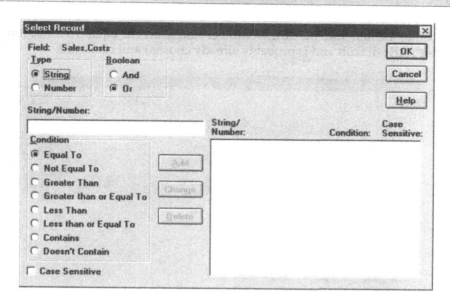

This is where you enter the criteria which must be met in order for records to be moved into the database.

The settings shown top left for Type and Boolean are fine. We'll search for a string – "halibut" – and the default Boolean 'Or' choice can be left alone.

❻ *Changing the Boolean setting to 'And' would mean that every criterion must be satisfied before a record can be imported. This setting is only useful if you define multiple criteria. 'Or' means that meeting a single criterion is sufficient to let a record through.* ❾

Enter 'halibut' into the String/Number slot; select the Equal To condition (this is the default and is probably already chosen) and click Add.

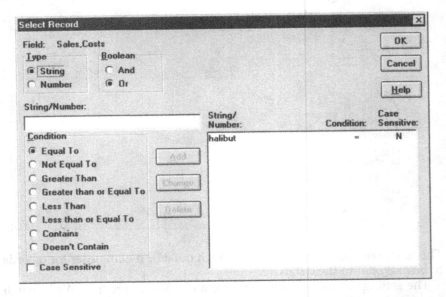

This puts in place a criterion which says "select a record if it contains the entry 'halibut' in the Products column".

❧ *As you can see, there are lots of other possibilities here. You could, for example, make the string case sensitive with the check box at the bottom left. Clearly this is inappropriate in this instance since the data contains the string 'Halibut' and we have just entered 'halibut'. However, you get the idea that you can build reasonably complex conditions with this dialog box.* ❧

When you've finished, click OK.

Validating a rules file

The validation process informs you whether the data load rules you have specified are correct, trapping errors before they get loose on your data. Click the 'Verify the current rules file' button.

❺ *If you followed this exercise to this point, you will have associated an outline during the allocation of field names. If you didn't do this, here you'll see a message about associating an outline before validation can take place. Click on the 'Associate an Outline with the current set of rules' button*

and choose the Fish:Basic:Basic outline. ❾

Hopefully you'll see a message like this.

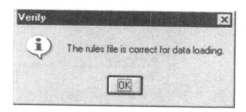

If not, a window giving details of errors appears and the information should point you towards the problem.

Check spellings, file delimiters, field names, that the chosen outline is correct and so on.

Saving a rules file

This is easy. Click the Save button and give the file a name.

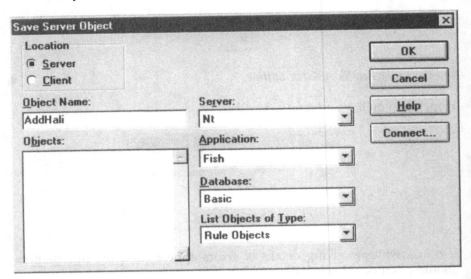

Ours is AddHali (there are eight characters at your disposal). Click OK, and it's now ready for use, or for copying for later modification and refinement.
   Close the Data Prep Editor.

Loading data with a rules file

Now we can perform the data load. Follow exactly the same steps as you did to load data straight from a text file: from the Application Manager menu, choose Database, Load Data and choose the data file `addfish.txt`. Click OK.

   Check the Use Rules box in the bottom left corner, and the Find... button alongside it. Select the Object AddHali, checking that Rule Objects are specified under List Objects of Type (bottom right).

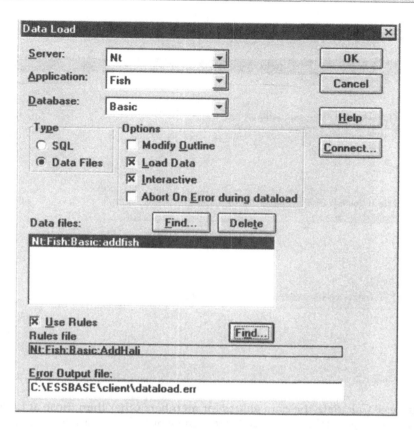

Note the name and location of the error output file. "But why?", you ask, "I successfully validated my Rules, didn't I?" Would that life was so simple. The validation ensures that the dimensions and members in the Rules file map to the dimensions and members in the outline, but it does not, unfortunately, guarantee that the data will load properly. Sigh.

Click OK, hold your breath, and –

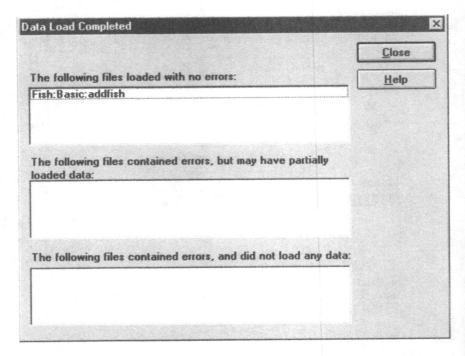

success! Calculate the data values for members other than those at Level 0 by choosing Database, Calculate from the Application Manager menu, and waltz off to Excel to look at the results.

Summary

During the course of this chapter, you have edited and extended an existing outline. You then identified a subset of data to be imported from a flat file by creating a Rules file. Data was loaded from the flat file in conjunction with the Rules file to place in the database just the records required. Note that the data has been 'appended' to the existing data, in other words, the existing data in the cube wasn't deleted.

Along the way you'll have seen some of the flexibility and power of the Application Manager, which is considerable. We're only able to scratch the surface of what this software can do, but by getting you started with importing and manipulating data, we hope to have helped you over the initial hurdles. We strongly recommend that you repeat the example given here, making a few changes and generally getting comfortable with the overall principle of loading data into a cube. When you are happy with this, start experimenting with the many other options that the Application Manager presents.

Solving problem three

Remember the three types of problem set out in Chapter 1? Well, you have now reached a stage where you are able to start work on building a solution to your very own Problem Three, questions that span multiple dimensions.

With data stored in a multi dimensional cube structure, you can interrogate it from the point of view of any of the dimensions. This can highlight correlations and identify trends previously unguessed, and this information can be used to determine the directions a business can take.

Chapter 19

Anchor dimensions and a few more concepts and pointers

Anchor dimensions

An anchor dimension is a dense dimension that is used by DB2 OLAP Server to define the structure in which the data is stored. DB2 OLAP Server will choose an anchor dimension for you automatically, but when you are planning a complex project, it's a task better performed by a thoughtful human than by a computer program. Choosing the right anchor dimension can reduce the amount of storage space required and speed data retrieval.

Anchor dimensions explained

Consider a table in which each dimension is represented by a column and in which the data from each combination of dimension values is held in a single column.

Assume that the value 1 in the MeasuresID column represents Profit, 2 represents Sales and 3, Costs. The value column holds the actual data for these measures. Thus for YearID 1 and ProductsID 1, the Profit is 26, the Sales 104 and the Costs 78.

YearID	ProductsID	MeasuresID	Value
1	1	1	26
1	1	2	104
1	1	3	78
1	2	1	18
1	2	2	52
1	2	3	34
1	3	1	8
and so on for many many rows.			

As you can see, there is a lot of repetitive information in each of the dimension columns, and the more dimensions there are the worse it gets. This brings with it a high overhead that adversely affects performance and is hungry of storage space.

One way to combat this is to pick one of the dimensions and use its members as column headings. This produces a table containing rather more data values per row, as shown below:

YearID	ProductsID	Profit	Sales	Costs
1	1	26	104	78
1	2	18	52	34
1	3	8	17	9
1	4	49	111	62
2	1	50	89	39
and so on but not for so many rows.				

Profit, Sales and Costs are all members of the Measures dimension, and instead of the Measures dimension figuring as a column, its three members undertake the role. This produces much less repetition and a much more compact table.

This table, in OLAP parlance, is a **fact table**. It's the main table in which your data is held. (There also exist **dimension tables** that hold member details for each of the other dimensions, Year and Products in this case).

In the above example, the Measures dimension has become the **anchor dimension** of the fact table.

Choosing an anchor dimension

There are several rules of thumb to guide you towards a sensible choice of anchor dimension:

- It must be a dense dimension
- The total number of members in the anchor dimension plus the total number of additional dimensions in the Essbase database must not exceed the maximum number of columns allowed in a table by the relational database
- It should have the largest number of members
- It should not need to gain further members
- It should not need any members to be deleted

Let's look at these points a little more closely.

- It must be a dense dimension

  We've already described dense dimensions as being ones for which large amounts of data exist. Accounts or Measures are classic dense dimensions and are very often chosen as the anchor dimension. If your database has an accounts dimension, it's the one you should consider first for the role of anchor dimension.

- The total number of members in the anchor dimension plus the total number of additional dimensions in the Essbase database must not exceed the maximum number of columns allowed in a table by the relational database

  This means just what is says. For DB2, the column limit is 500. Our tiny example barely scrapes into existence with a total of five, but do your own sums for your real data.

- It should have the largest number of members

  The anchor dimension should contain the largest number of members possible within the column limit of the relational database. If you've two dense dimensions, choose the one with the largest number of members.

- It should not need to gain further members
- It should not need any members to be deleted

  Once you have loaded data into a database, you cannot change or delete the anchor dimension unless you clear out all the data within. With a large database, this can be a time-consuming task.

It was impressed upon us by IBMers (who really do know about these things) that it is important to get the anchor dimension right early on in the project as it can be difficult to change later.

Inspecting an anchor dimension

To see which dimension has been specified as the anchor dimension, select a database in the Server window. We'll look at Fish:Basic. From the

Database menu, choose Information, and in the Database Information dialog, click the Run-time tab.

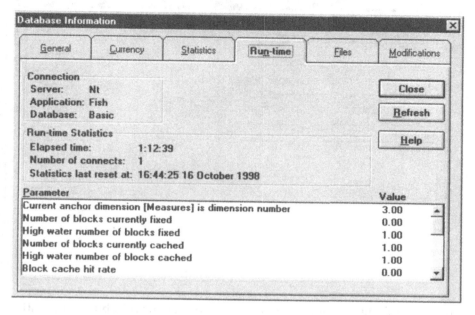

In the list of Parameter settings, you'll see the current anchor dimension is Measures, and this choice has been made automatically. (The value '3.00' correlates to the DB2 table that holds an identifying number for each dimension; we inspected this table in Chapter 17).

Defining an anchor dimension

This should be done after finalizing the outline but before any data is loaded.

In the Application Manager, open the Outline Editor to show the outline for the Fish:Basic database. Highlight the dimension you wish to declare as the anchor dimension; just for demonstration purposes, we'll change it from Measures to Year, so highlight Year in the outline.

Click the 'Define the attributes for the selected member' button.

In the Dimension Specification dialog, click the User Attributes tab.

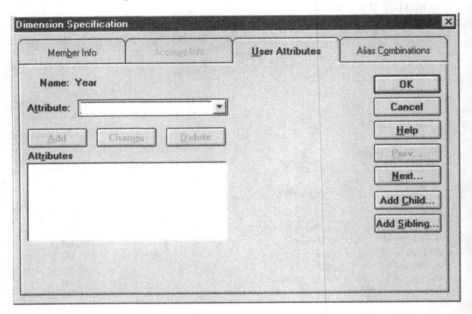

In the Attribute slot, type 'RELANCHOR' and click the Add button beneath. RELANCHOR now appears as an attribute of Year.

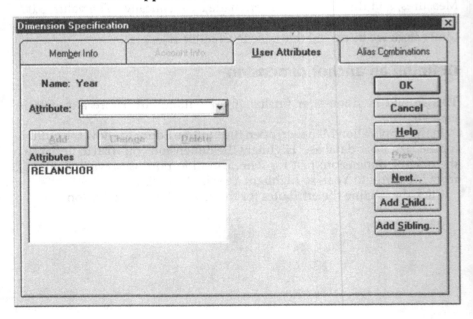

Click OK. You have just set a User Defined Attribute (UDA) for the member Year in the Fish:Basic outline, and this is now shown in the outline. (UDAs can be made visible or invisible by selecting or deselecting Attributes in the View menu).

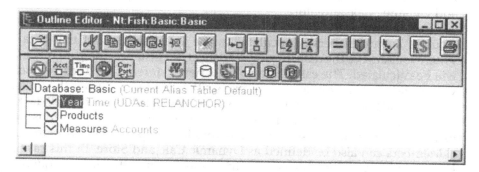

When you close the outline, you'll be prompted to save the modification. If you say yes, you'll see an Essbase error message telling you that 'The system selected anchor dimension [Measures] cannot be replaced by a user-specified anchor dimension with data loaded'. This is saying, in a slightly cryptic fashion, that the current anchor dimension, selected automatically by Essbase ('the system') cannot be replaced by the one you've just specified because the database is already loaded with data. As we said above, anchor dimensions cannot be changed or deleted without clearing out all of the data.

Here this outcome is fine because we don't really want to change the anchor dimension. Click OK in the error message dialog, and reply no when asked, on closing the Outline Editor, whether you wish to save the outline.

A few more concepts and pointers

We've only shown you the barest minimum of what you can do with DB2 OLAP Server. When you start building applications for real, more new terms and concepts will surface. So that you are at least able to recognize them, below is a brief explanation of some of the most fundamental.

Dynamic calculations

It's possible to improve the calculation performance of a database by making use of dynamic calculations. There are two types: Dynamic Calc and Dynamic Calc and Store.

Members can be defined as having a dynamic calculation, and the data value of such members is calculated at the time you request that data. When you retrieve the data into a spreadsheet, for instance, these members will be calculated. The calculated value is never stored, so that each time you retrieve it, it is re-calculated. This has the effect of reducing the time taken to calculate the whole database, but can lead to increased data retrieval time. Dynamic calculation of members in dense dimensions is usually very fast and consequently has very little impact on performance.

Members can also be defined as Dynamic Calc and Store. In this case, Essbase calculates the values on retrieval and stores them. Subsequent retrievals do not perform the calculation again (unless Essbase detects a need to do so) and are therefore quicker.

There is, as with most tuning techniques, an element of compromise to be struck between your needs for a fast response for users, a shorter time taken to back up, the disk space used and other factors. When performance becomes an issue with your database, this is an area that would repay study; here we can only make you aware of its existence and potential importance.

Partitioning

Partitioning is another important technique for reducing the size of a database, improving the efficiency with which resources are used and improving performance generally.

As the term suggests, it's all about dividing a database into pieces which can then be shared by other databases. Partitioning comes into play when you're working with more than one application; you can define partitions between different databases in different applications, either on the same computer or on different ones.

It's well beyond the scope of a first trial run, so again we'll just point to it as an area for future study if the need arises.

Calculating size

With multi-dimensional databases, size can be a problem, and bigger is often not at all better. At the planning stage, effort put into separating the data that's necessary from the data that would just take up space and add no information of value is effort well expended. This is not just a matter of what data is available, it's also about who will be questioning the database and what sorts of questions they will be asking.

We said in Chapter 13 that OLAP cubes grow dramatically in size as members and dimensions are added. For example, given a year's worth of sales from a single store selling 20 products, youd have approximately 300 * 20 = 6,000 intersections. Given 25 stores, you'd have 6,000 * 25 = 150,000. In fact, the number is likely to be larger than this rather crude estimate because this one only takes account of the leaf node data. As you add members to the hierarchy (grouping days into months, months into quarters, quarters into years etc.) you increase the number of possible intersections.

The bottom line is that multi-dimensional databases can grow to be huge, so it is important to ensure that only vital data is stored.

Calc Script Editor

A calculation script, called a calc script for short, is a series of commands, equations and formulae. Most common calculations can be performed from the outline (using consolidation objects) but there are some mathematical operations that lie outwith its capabilities. In such cases, you can define a calc script that applies the necessary formulae. The script is saved and then run against the database at the time the database is calculated; you simple choose a calc script to run (instead of the default which simply processes the calculations specified in the outline).

The button to access the Calc Script Editor is the second from the left in the Server window, looking like this:

You can be very smart with these, but probably won't need to be so for a while.

Reports

There is a report generation tool, but it's not fab. It's the sort of thing that produces those yellowing stacks of continuous paper that we've all seen lying forlorn on window sills, chairs and on the floor in the corner. Output is plain unadorned text, good only for the most basic tasks or for huge volumes that run overnight. Given the excellent hooks into spreadsheet programs and other reporting tools, you're much better off using the reporting facilities they offer.

You reach this antediluvian from the third button in the Server window:

Chapter 20

Visual Warehouse and DB2 OLAP Server symbiosis

Bringing it all together

We've shown you how to get started with Visual Warehouse and DB2 OLAP Server. We have tended to treat these two tools as if they were separate, and that is how they initially appear. However, it has become clear from our conversations with people at IBM that many of their customers eventually end up using the tools very tightly together. In other words, they use the scheduling power of Visual Warehouse's Business Views to drive DB2 OLAP Server. Indeed, some IBM customers buy DB2 OLAP Server and then come back a few months later and buy Visual Warehouse simply in order to schedule the operation of their OLAP cube.

Since the whole aim of this book has been to get you started as rapidly as possible, we haven't covered this aspect, but it is worth bearing in mind as you learn more about the tools.

Last words

That's it. We gained huge enjoyment from writing this book and we hope you had as much fun in using it. Given the power of these products, there is a whole lot more to be learnt, but that is another way of saying that there is a whole lot more fun to be had. We hope you find that enjoyment and go on to achieve great things with Visual Warehouse and DB2 OLAP Server.

Overview of data warehousing

This appendix expands on the definitions of Data Warehousing and Business Intelligence that were presented in Chapter 1. There is a small degree of overlap between the two sections, but it seems acceptable because it allows both sections to be read independently.

Data warehouses

Q: What is the definition of a data warehouse?
A: A can of worms.

This isn't meant to imply that data warehouses are cans of worms, just that defining them usually leads to fist fights. This is probably because:

- the field is still young and poorly defined
- everyone wants to make their mark on the field by producing a slightly different definition

So, instead of a neat, clean definition which will add to the growing list of definitions, here is a brief potted history that tries to explain what a data warehouse is in terms of what you can expect to get out of one.

Background

The process of computerization within a company is often gradual. Perhaps the payroll is computerized first, then perhaps the stock control, later the ordering system and so on. This incremental method has the major advantage of being manageable – simultaneously computerizing every facet of data handling within an entire company is a terrifying thought. On the other hand, the incremental method usually means that the computer systems are purchased from different companies with little thought for compatibility or integration. Mergers between different companies are becoming increasingly common and that process also tends to increase rather than decrease the number of disparate database systems within the company.

No-one is suggesting that this computer-evolution within a company is unreasonable; the very fact that it is common suggests that it's a successful strategy; perhaps those companies that tried for the simultaneous solution are no longer with us. However, the legacy of this incremental system acquisition is a set of problems (sorry, challenges) which are also common to many companies.

Challenges

As computerization continues to advance, people are, quite reasonably, expecting to be able to extract more information from the computer systems in their companies. By 'more information' we mean that they want answers to questions like 'Which of our sales people is the most productive?' or 'Which of our products are really the most profitable, taking all factors (including shipping costs, wastage, theft, promotions, staff training and advertizing) into account?' Given that people know that all of these factors are carefully logged somewhere within the company's databases, it seems perfectly reasonable to ask such questions. And it is. In fact, asking the questions doesn't present a problem; answering them, on the other hand....

We need a name for questions like this to distinguish them from more mundane ones like 'What is Fred Smith's telephone number?'. There doesn't seem to be a good generic term, so we'll call them 'broad' questions. We toyed with more sophisticated terms like 'trend', 'analytical', 'summation' but, as you can see from the examples below, none of these terms is broad enough, hence our choice.

Questions that span time

Suppose that you are a senior manager in a retail company. You might ask a question like 'Show me the sales of dog food as totals per month, for the last five years'. This seems like an innocent question, but may not be. Suppose, for example, that your sales database logs every single customer transaction and that you have, for the sake of argument, 50 stores with 20 checkouts per store. Given, say, an average customer transaction time of 2 minutes, you can expect five years worth of data to be about 300,000,000 records, so in order to answer your question the database has to look at each and every one. And it gets worse. Since every customer transaction is likely to involve the purchase of much more than just dog food, the database has also to look at other records (stored in other tables) which contain the details of the transaction. The end result may be a query that takes several days to answer. This sounds bad, but think about the rest of the system. Either people are entering current data manually, or it is being updated electronically. Either way, the danger is that your query will slow the entire system to a crawl leading to frustrated employees and/or customers. Incidentally, even apparently simpler questions like 'Show me the total number of cans of dog food sold over the last five years' are equally damaging.

That's one class of dangerous question. Another is one that asks for data that resides on two or more database systems.

Questions that span disparate data sources

Suppose that your company doesn't pay its sales force by commission, but rather gives each person an individually negotiated wage. You decide to find out which of your sales people are the most cost effective, so you ask to see their salary plotted against the sales they have gained. Unfortunately the sales information is kept in one database and the salary information in another. The two databases have no direct means of communicating, so someone has to process the request by querying the two databases separately and combining the answers. This in itself can be a time-consuming process, but for a single request it isn't too bad. The problem is that you, and other people, are likely to make multiple requests of this kind. If they are all handled individually, then one (or more) people will be spending all of their time processing such queries.

And the number of possible transfers is unsettling. Suppose that your company has five different database systems. The number of possible data transfers is 5*4=20. Given ten databases, the number rises to 10*9=90. We aren't suggesting that you are likely to want to move data along all of the possible routes. However, since each route is likely to present a unique set of problems, the effort involved in moving data around in the company rapidly becomes very high even for a small proportion of the possible moves.

❝ In fact, here we have just touched upon the problems and have quoted just a few relatively trivial examples. There are whole books devoted to this topic; an excellent one is Bill (W.H.) Inmon's "Building the Data Warehouse" (Wiley-QED, ISBN 0-471-56960-7). We heartily recommend this to anyone who feels the need to *be further convinced. However, we suspect that, if the examples given above hit a nerve, then you may already be sufficiently convinced to read on.* **9**

Solutions

Data warehousing has been developed as a way of addressing these sorts of problem, which we can look at sequentially.

Questions that span time

At its simplest, a data warehouse is a copy of an operational database held on a separate machine. This copy is updated at regular intervals, say, once a week. The update takes place during a 'slack' time on the operational system, at weekends or during the night. All operational transactions are performed, as before, on the original database. All of the 'broad' queries are run against the data warehouse copy. While it is true that the data warehouse will contain data which is up to a week out of date, most broad questions are not time-sensitive enough for this to be a major problem.

The type of data warehouse described above is very easy to set up and stops the performance interference between the operational and historical data. However, the broad questions can still take several days to answer. There are essentially two reasons for the time taken, and both can be addressed by modifying the copy of the data in the data warehouse.

1. For a start, data in an operational database is structured in such a way as to ensure that it is very compact. In addition, it is also structured in such a way that the data is both easy to enter and difficult to damage. (As a trivial example, the address of each of your customers will typically be stored only once in the database. Thus, when they place a new order, the employee who is entering the data can choose the address, rather than type it in. This saves time and also removes the possibility that the employee will misspell the address.)

   So, the structure of an operational database is optimized for data entry. When a copy of that data is placed in the data warehouse, it is perfectly possible to restructure it, this time optimizing it for data retrieval. One of the few drawbacks of this re-structuring is that the volume of the data can expand dramatically during this process, but since disk space is now so cheap this isn't so much of a problem as it used to be.

6 *While we are on the subject of the difference between operational databases and data warehouses, it is clear that operational systems often contain historical data going back for years which is essentially never updated. One further advantage of a data* *warehouse is that, once it has been established, it is often possible to delete some of the 'historical' data from the operational system after moving it permanently to the data warehouse. This may, in turn, speed the operational database considerably.* ❯

2. The second reason why broad questions take a long time to answer is that they typically look at all of the data and ask for some kind of summary of that data. It is a central tenet of an operational database that summary information is never stored. This may sounds odd until you think about it. The data in an operational database is there to be examined, added to and altered, so any summary information that is stored therein will rapidly become unreliable. Of course, the data in a data warehouse is simply there so that it can be queried. This means that it isn't subject to change, so it suddenly makes eminent sense to calculate summaries and store them. Going back to the dog food example for a moment, when the data is imported into the data warehouse, we might calculate the weekly sales for all of the items and store this information. When the dog food question is asked, instead of 300,000,000+ records, the query will only need to look 52*5=260 records. Thus questions can come back from a data warehouse in seconds rather than days. Of course, a delicate and intelligent balance has to be struck here. If the data warehouse is told to pre-calculate all possible values, it will become truly massive and take forever to be created. So, the designers of the data warehouse need to talk to the people who will be using it, find out what questions are likely to be asked, and choose the best values to pre-calculate. This is often an iterative process.

❮ *This concept of storing 'pre-digested' data can be used in another way. Broad questions rarely require data at the finest level of detail. For example, you wouldn't really expect a manager to ask to see the entire list of purchases made by John Wilkins on March 3rd 1992. So, there are times when it is may be desirable to store only summaries of the original data in the data warehouse, rather than all of it. (This isn't meant to imply that all of the original, highly detailed, data would be thrown away. Only someone who was incredibly brave/foolhardy would do that. We would always, unless there were very compelling reasons, ensure that such data was held in its entirety on some form of backup medium such as tape.)* ❯

Questions that span disparate data sources

If your company has, say, two operational databases, a data warehouse can make even more sense. You move data from both databases into the same data warehouse and there you can perform whatever correlations you like. Simple; at least in theory. In practice, this can be a lot of work. One of the main problems is that data in different databases is often incompatible.

As a simple example, consider names. One database might store them in one field as 'M.Whitehorn', another might store them in two fields as 'Mark' 'Whitehorn'.

Dates are also a major source of problems. One system may store them as text characters '4 July 1998' another as text characters in US format '7/4/1998', a third in UK format '4/7/98', another as a numerical value '35980' and so on. The list is nearly endless. When these are brought together in a data warehouse, it is essential that they are all transformed into the same format.

And you can never relax. We were once caught out by two systems that stored dates in an identical fashion. Despite this, we occasionally noted errors associated with processing dates in the data warehouse. It took us some time to realize that the first system assumed that Sunday was the first day of the week, while the second assumed that it was Monday....

None of these problems is insurmountable. We just mention them to make the point that the term 'simple' as used above refers to the theory. In practice, correlating data from disparate database needs time, thought, expertise and intelligence. However, it can reward the hard work many times over.

As we said before, the more database systems your company has, the more possible interactions you may need. A data warehouse keeps the number of transfers to a minimum. For example, given 10 databases there are 45 possible paths down which you may want to move data. If you put a data warehouse in place, the total possible routes drops dramatically to 10.

❻ *Before anyone else points it out, we suppose we'd better come clean and say that these figures are impressive because we are talking about reasonable numbers of operational databases. Given a low number, like two, a data warehouse actually increases the number of possible transfers. The break-even value is three, and the data warehouse starts winning at 4 and above. However, we aren't advocating this as the only reason to use a data warehouse, we are simply saying that it is often one of the fringe benefits. And indeed, when you buy data warehousing tools like Visual Warehouse, you will get tools that are specifically designed to move data into the data warehouse. So, even when the number of transfers is greater, the difficulty of actually moving the data is decreased.* ❾

Summary so far, plus some additional information

Creating and maintaining a data warehouse is simple in theory.

The 'data warehouse' in physical terms is likely to be a separate machine, running perhaps DB2 on NT.

In order to create a functional data warehouse:

1. First there is consultation between those who will build it and those who will use it.
2. Then data is moved from the operational database into the data warehouse.
3. (During this process the data is often summarized and transformed.)
4. The users of the data warehouse are then given access to the data in the data warehouse.
5. The data in the data warehouse is then updated at regular intervals.
6. The data warehouse is then modified as required to suit the users' changing requirements.

This all sounds very easy, and you could be forgiven for wondering why you actually need to buy a product like Visual Warehouse. After all, it isn't likely to help with the consultation part. As for the other functions, like moving the data out of the operational database, surely any competent database administrator can do that?

The answer to this is 'Yes, you're right.' Given a very simple database and data warehouse you don't need Visual Warehouse or indeed any other data warehousing tool. So what is Visual Warehouse for? What does it do?

The answer is that most databases aren't simple and neither are most data warehouses. Experience has shown that moving data from an operational database to a data warehouse isn't too much of a problem.

Of the steps outlined above, the ones that typically turn out to be difficult, complex and time consuming are:

- The consultation between those who will build it and those who will use it.
- Summarizing and transforming the data as it is moved.
- Automating the update of the data in the data warehouse at regular intervals.
- Documenting the entire process so that it can be modified.
- Modifying the data warehouse as required to suit the users' changing requirements.

Visual Warehouse doesn't help with the consultation (you are actually going to have to talk to each other, painful as this may be). On the other hand, Visual Warehouse is specifically designed to help with all of the others.

Essentially it is a tool which enables you to do the following:

- Set up and control the database which will hold the data warehouse.
- Set up and maintain the connections between the operational databases and the data warehouse.
- Set up and maintain the transfer of data between the operational databases and the data warehouse.
- Set up and maintain the transformation of the data as it is transferred.
- Provide a host of options for automating these processes.
- Lastly, but by no means leastly, it provides a framework which 'documents' how the data warehouse is being maintained. This means that modifying the data warehouse is much easier, and also makes the handover of the data warehouse (as IT personnel change) much easier.

Appendix 2

IBM's Business Intelligence solution

Visual Warehouse and DB2 OLAP Server are only two of the Business Intelligence tools offered by IBM. What follows is a very brief outline of the other elements in the Business Intelligence family.

Visual Warehouse & DB2 OLAP Server

Visual Warehouse comes in four flavors, one of which is vanilla – simply Visual Warehouse and nothing else. IBM has numerous business partners – Cognos, Business Objects and Brio are amongst those that offer front-end visualization and data access tools for Visual Warehouse. A Cognos Edition, a Business Objects Edition and a Brio Edition of Visual Warehouse are both available.

DB2 OLAP Server is also offered in four flavors: in plain vanilla or with the extra visualization and access functionality offered by the Cognos Edition, Business Objects Edition and Brio Edition.

DataJoiner

As the name suggests, DataJoiner is all about working with data from disparate sources, and maximizing the usefulness of such data stores can be fundamental to an organization's data handling strategy.

Supported sources include Oracle, Sybase, Microsoft SQL Server, IMS & VSAM. Amongst DataJoiner's many features are support for heterogeneous joins and a database access optimizer.

ETI*Extract

ETI*Extract and Vality Integrity (mentioned below) are data transformation and cleansing tools and both come from IBM partners. ETI*Extract performs complex and highly customizable filtering, derivation and summarization tasks with support for a broad range of data sources.

Vality Integrity

Another data transformation and cleansing tool, focusing on data typing, fuzzy matching and hidden values.

Intelligent Miner for Data

This is a suite of tools for identifying and extracting business intelligence from the data available.

The term "data mining" describes the process of extracting worthwhile information from stored data, information that was previously hidden in the mass of data. Data mining can lead to a more intimate understanding of an organization, and that knowledge can be used to improve performance.

Intelligent Miner can help in many ways; for instance, it can be implemented by the marketing department to target the right customers with the right information, and by the finance department to spot fraud.

Intelligent Miner for Text

Another suite of data mining tools, aimed at extracting information from text. Tools include an advanced search engine and tools to enable text out on the Web to be searched.

Net.Data

This tool, which comes with DB2, supports Web access to relational and flat file data on platforms including DB2, databases enabled to use DataJoiner and ODBC data sources.

DataPropagator Relational & DataPropagator NonRelational

This tool provides data replication capabilities and are integrated into DB2 Universal Database and DataJoiner. The replication facilities permit the capture of changes in source databases for inclusion in a data warehouse. The NonRelational version is for use with IMS databases.

Data Refresher

Data from non-relational databases and files, such as IMS and VSAM, can be captured and transformed using this application.

Appendix 3

The software

On the CD-ROM supplied with this book you will find a limited use (60 days from installation) version of Visual Warehouse which you are welcome to install and use to try out the examples described in this book. You are, of course, welcome to use the product in any other way that the IBM licence agreement allows.

If you want to install Visual Warehouse from the CD-ROM, pop it into your CD-ROM drive and follow the on-screen instructions. Note that, before Visual Warehouse can be installed, you need to have DB2 in place. A trial version of DB2 can be obtained from the IBM Web site:

```
http://www.software.ibm.com/data/db2
```

Alternatively, there is a trial copy of DB2 on the CD-ROM contained in our earlier book: *DB2 for Windows NT – Fast.*

A sample copy of DB2 OLAP can be obtained from:

```
http://www.software.ibm.com/data/db2olapcode
```

Sample files

The sample files mentioned in the book are located on the enclosed CD-ROM in a folder called SAMPLES. These include:

```
AddFish.txt
Fish.txt
Sales.txt
TooFoo.txt
```

Also in this folder are some HTML files kindly supplied by Alan Carpenter. These extend the information given in this book and are well worth reading.

The front-end tools described in Chapter 4 are located in the folder DB24NTF (DB2 For NT Fast). The credit for coding these tools belongs to Jonny Black (University of Dundee) and it is his voice that speaks to you from the highly informative readme files that are included.

Also included within this folder are the data generation tools that we provide with the DB2 book. These were originally written for a magazine called *PC User* in the UK. The publishing house which owned *PC User*, emap, has kindly agreed to allow us to include the code and sample tables on the CD-ROM. Jonny Black tidied up my rather ratty code, and it is included in one of the sub-directories underneath DB24NTF.

Overview of data warehouse components

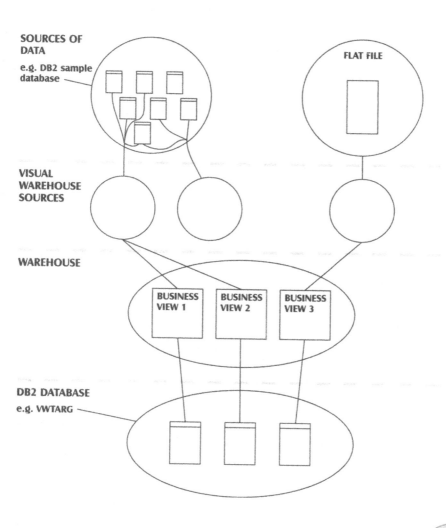

SOURCES OF DATA

e.g. DB2 sample database

FLAT FILE

VISUAL WAREHOUSE SOURCES

WAREHOUSE

BUSINESS VIEW 1

BUSINESS VIEW 2

BUSINESS VIEW 3

DB2 DATABASE

e.g. VWTARG

Index